NIA / PENINSULA GOLF CLUB, SAN MATEO, 1923 / *COLORADO* / BROADMOOR GOLF CLUB, COLORADO SPRINGS, 1918 /
RTFORD GOLF CLUB, WEST HARTFORD, 1946 / SHENNECOSSET COUNTRY CLUB, GROTON, 1916 / WAMPANOAG COUNTR
PAL GOLF COURSE, SARASOTA, 1927 / BOCA RATON GOLF CLUB, BOCA RATON, 1925 / BRENTWOOD GOLF CLUB, JACKS
TRY CLUB, JACKSONVILLE, 1922 / FORT GEORGE ISLAND GOLF CLUB, JACKSONVILLE, 1922 / FORT MYERS GOLF AND
NTRY CLUB, KEYSTONE HEIGHTS, 1927 / LAKE WALES COUNTRY CLUB, LAKE WALES, 1925 / MELBOURNE GOLF CLUB, MIAMI COUNTRY CLUB,
LUB, PALM BEACH, 1917 / PALMA CEIA GOLF CLUB, TAMPA, 1923 / PALMA SOLA GOLF CLUB, GRADENTOWN, 1924 / PANAMA COUNTRY CLUB, LYNN HAVEN, 1927 /
UB OF ORLANDO, ORLANDO, 1918 / RIVIERA COUNTRY CLUB, CORAL GABLES, 1924 / SAN JOSE COUNTRY CLUB, JACKSONVILLE, 1925 / SARA BAY COUNTRY CLUB,
23 / UNIVERSITY OF FLORIDA GOLF CLUB, GAINESVILLE, 1921 / *GEORGIA* / ATHENS COUNTRY CLUB, ATHENS, 1926 / AUGUSTA COUNTRY CLUB, AUGUSTA, 1927 /
COLUMBUS, 1915 / EAST LAKE COUNTRY CLUB, ATLANTA, 1915 / FORREST HILLS GOLF CLUB, AUGUSTA, 1926 / HIGHLAND COUNTRY CLUB, LAGRANGE, 1922 /
H RESORT AND COUNTRY CLUB, SAVANNAH, 1927 / WALTHOUR GOLF COURSE, SAVANNAH, 1928 / WASHINGTON WILKES GOLF CLUB, WASHINGTON, 1928 / *ILLINOIS*
SKOKIE, 1917 / EXMOOR COUNTRY CLUB, HIGHLAND PARK, 1914 / HINSDALE GOLF CLUB, HINSDALE, 1913 / INDIAN HILL CLUB, WINNETKA, 1914 / NORTHMOOR
D, 1915 / SKOKIE COUNTRY CLUB, GLENCOE, 1915 / *INDIANA* / BROADMOOR COUNTRY CLUB, INDIANAPOLIS, 1921 / FAIRVIEW GOLF CLUB, FORT WAYNE, 1927 /
NTUCKY / IDLE HOUR COUNTRY CLUB, LEXINGTON, 1924 / *MAINE* / AUGUSTA COUNTRY CLUB, MANCHESTER, 1916 / BIDDEFORD SACO COUNTRY CLUB, SACO, 1921 /
BORS, 1922 / PARADISE SPRINGS GOLF CLUB, PARADISE SPRINGS, 1920 / PENOBSCOT VALLEY COUNTRY CLUB, BANGOR, 1923 / POLAND SPRINGS COUNTRY CLUB,
N ECHO, 1924 / CHEVY CHASE COUNTRY CLUB, CHEVY CHASE, 1915 / CONGRESSIONAL COUNTRY CLUB, BETHESDA, 1930 / INDIAN SPRING COUNTRY CLUB, LAUREL,
UTH, 1914 / BELMONT COUNTRY CLUB, BELMONT, 1918 / BRAE BURN COUNTRY CLUB, WEST NEWTON, 1912 / CHARLES RIVER COUNTRY CLUB, NEWTON CENTRE,
ATHOL, 1927 / ESSEX COUNTY CLUB, MANCHESTER, 1909 / GEORGE WRIGHT MUNICIPAL GOLF COURSE, BOSTON, 1931 / GREENOCK COUNTRY CLUB, LEE, 1927 /
COUNTRY CLUB OF NEW BEDFORD, DARTMOUTH, 1924 / NANTUCKET GOLF CLUB, NANTUCKET, 1917 / NEWTON COMMONWEALTH, NEWTON, 1921 / NORTH ANDOVER
SOUTH HADLEY, 1922 / OYSTER HARBORS CLUB, OSTERVILLE, 1927 / COUNTRY CLUB OF PITTSFIELD, PITTSFIELD, 1921 / PLYMOUTH COUNTRY CLUB, PLYMOUTH,
ND, 1924 / SPRINGFIELD COUNTRY CLUB, SPRINGFIELD, 1924 / TATNUCK COUNTRY CLUB, WORCESTER, 1930 / TEKOA COUNTRY CLUB, WESTFIELD, 1923 / TOYTOWN
UB, WALTHAM, 1921 / WELLESLEY COUNTRY CLUB, WELLESLEY, 1910 / WESTON GOLF CLUB, WESTON, 1916 / WHALING CITY COUNTRY CLUB, NEW BEDFORD, 1920
AUBURNDALE, 1927 / WORCESTER COUNTRY CLUB, WORCESTER, 1913 / WYCKOFF PARK GOLF CLUB, HOLYOKE, 1923 / *MICHIGAN* / BARTON HILLS COUNTRY CLUB,
916 / ELK GRAND RAPIDS GOLF CLUB, ELK RAPIDS, 1923 / FRANKLIN HILLS COUNTRY CLUB, FRANKLIN, 1926 / FRED WARDELL ESTATE GOLF CLUB, DETROIT, 1920
ROE GOLF AND COUNTRY CLUB, MONROE, 1919 / MUSKEGON COUNTRY CLUB, MUSKEGON, 1911 / OAKLAND HILLS COUNTRY CLUB, BIRMINGHAM, 1917 / RACKHAM
RY CLUB, ST. CLAIR, 1923 / WARREN VALLEY GOLF CLUB, DEARBORN, 1927 / WESTERN GOLF AND COUNTRY CLUB, REDFORD, 1926 / *MINNESOTA* / INTERLACHEN
WHITE BEAR YACHT CLUB, WHITE BEAR LAKE, 1912 / WOODHILL COUNTRY CLUB, WAYZATA, 1916 / *MISSOURI* / HILLCREST COUNTRY CLUB, KANSAS CITY, 1917 /
CH, 1912 / BETHLEHEM COUNTRY CLUB, BETHLEHEM, 1910 / CARTER COUNTRY CLUB, LEBANON, 1923 / KINGSWOOD COUNTRY CLUB, WOLFEBORO, 1926 / LAKE
BETHLEHEM, 1914 / MT. WASHINGTON GOLF CLUB, BRETTON WOODS, 1915 / TORY PINES RESORT, FRANCESTOWN, 1929 / WENTWORTH-BY-THE-SEA, PORTSMOUTH,
, 1924 / HOMESTEAD COUNTRY CLUB, SPRING LAKE, 1920 / KNICKERBOCKER COUNTRY CLUB, TENAFLY, 1915 / LONE PINE GOLF CLUB, VERONA, 1925 / MONTCLAIR
, RIDGEWOOD, 1916 / RIVERTON COUNTRY CLUB, RIVERTON, 1916 / SEAVIEW COUNTRY CLUB, ABSECON, 1915 / *NEW YORK* / BELLEVUE COUNTRY CLUB, SYRACUSE,
A GOLF CLUB, CHAUTAUQUA, 1921 / ELMSFORD COUNTRY CLUB, ELMSFORD, 1919 / FAIRVIEW COUNTRY CLUB, ELMSFORD, 1920 / FOX HILLS GOLF CLUB, STATEN
MARK TWAIN GOLF COURSE, ELMIRA, 1937 / MONROE GOLF CLUB, PITTSFORD, 1923 / OAK HILL COUNTRY CLUB, ROCHESTER, 1923 / RIP VAN WINKLE COUNTRY
BRONXVILLE, 1914 / TEUGEGA COUNTRY CLUB, ROME, 1920 / THENDARA GOLF CLUB, THENDARA, 1921 / TUPPER LAKE COUNTRY CLUB, TUPPER LAKE, 1915 /
ASHEVILLE COUNTRY CLUB, ASHEVILLE, 1928 / BENVENUE COUNTRY CLUB, ROCKY MOUNT, 1922 / BILTMORE FOREST COUNTRY CLUB, ASHEVILLE, 1921 / BLOWING
AND COUNTRY CLUB, CHARLOTTE, 1928 / CAROLINA PINES GOLF CLUB, RALEIGH, 1932 / CATAWBA COUNTRY CLUB, HICKORY, 1946 / CHARLOTTE COUNTRY CLUB,
DERSONVILLE COUNTRY CLUB, HENDERSONVILLE, 1925 / HIGHLAND COUNTRY CLUB, FAYETTEVILLE, 1945 / HIGHLANDS COUNTRY CLUB, HIGHLANDS, 1926 / HOPE
SA HILLS GOLF CLUB, MORGANTOWN, 1928 / MONROE GOLF CLUB, MONROE, 1927 / MOORE PARK GOLF CLUB, MOORESVILLE, 1948 / MYERS PARK COUNTRY CLUB,
UNTRY CLUB NO. 1, PINEHURST, 1900 / PINEHURST COUNTRY CLUB NO. 2, PINEHURST, 1901 / PINEHURST COUNTRY CLUB NO. 3, PINEHURST, 1907 / PINEHURST

COUNTRY CLUB NO. 4, PINEHURST, 1912 / PINEHURST COUNTRY CLUB NO. 5, PINEHURST, 1927 / RALEIGH COUNTRY CLUB, RALEIGH, 1947 / RICHMOND PINES COUN CLUB, ROCKINGHAM, 1926 / ROARING GAP GOLF CLUB, ROARING GAP, 1925 / COUNTRY CLUB OF SALISBURY, SALISBURY, 1927 / SEDGEFIELD COUNTRY C GREENSBORO, 1924 / SOUTHERN PINES COUNTRY CLUB, SOUTHERN PINES, 1923 / STRYKER GOLF CLUB, FAYETTEVILLE, 1946 / TRYON COUNTRY CLUB, TRYON, 19 WILMINGTON MUNICIPAL GOLF COURSE, WILMINGTON, 1925 / WAYNESVILLE COUNTRY CLUB, WAYNESVILLE, 1924 / *OHIO* / ACACIA COUNTRY CLUB, LYNDHURST, 19 ALADDIN COUNTRY CLUB, COLUMBUS, 1921 / ATHENS COUNTRY CLUB, ATHENS, 1921 / BROOKSIDE COUNTRY CLUB, CANTON, 1922 / COLUMBUS COUNTRY C COLUMBUS, 1914 / CONGRESS LAKE CLUB, HARTVILLE, 1929 / DAYTON GOLF & COUNTRY CLUB, DAYTON, 1919 / DELAWARE GOLF CLUB, DELAWARE, 1922 / ELKS COU CLUB OF COLUMBUS, COLUMBUS, 1921 / GRANVILLE GOLF CLUB, GRANVILLE, 1924 / HAMILTON ELKS COUNTRY CLUB, HAMILTON, 1925 / HAWTHORNE VALLEY COU CLUB, SOLON, 1926 / HYDE PARK GOLF AND COUNTRY CLUB, CINCINNATI, 1927 / INVERNESS CLUB, TOLEDO, 1920 / LANCASTER COUNTRY CLUB, LANCASTER, 19 MAKETEWAH COUNTRY CLUB, CINCINNATI, 1919 / MANAKIKI GOLF CLUB, WILLOUGHBY, 1928 / MIAMI SHORES GOLF CLUB, TROY, 1926 / MILL CREEK PARK GOLF CL YOUNGSTOWN, 1928 / MOHAWK GOLF CLUB, TIFFIN, 1917 / OAKWOOD COUNTRY CLUB, CLEVELAND, 1915 / PIQUA COUNTRY CLUB, PIQUA, 1920 / PORTSMITH C COUNTRY CLUB, MCDERMOTT, 1920 / SCIOTO COUNTRY CLUB, COLUMBUS, 1916 / SHAKER HEIGHTS COUNTRY CLUB, SHAKER HEIGHTS, 1913 / SPRINGFIELD COUN CLUB, SPRINGFIELD, 1921 / WESTBROOK COUNTRY CLUB, MANSFIELD, 1920 / WILLOWICK COUNTRY CLUB, CLEVELAND, 1917 / WYANDOT MUNICIPAL GOLF COUR WORTHINGTON, 1922 / YOUNGSTOWN COUNTRY CLUB, YOUNGSTOWN, 1921 / ZANEVILLE COUNTRY CLUB, ZANEVILLE, 1932 / *PENNSYLVANIA* / ALLEGHENY COUNTRY C SEWICKLEY, 1923 / ARONIMINK GOLF CLUB, NEWTOWN SQUARE, 1928 / BEDFORD SPRINGS HOTEL, BEDFORD SPRINGS, 1924 / BUCK HILL GOLF CLUB, BUCK HILL FA 1922 / CEDARBROOK COUNTRY CLUB, BLUE BELL, 1921 / EDGEWOOD COUNTRY CLUB, PITTSBURGH, 1921 / ELKVIEW GOLF CLUB, CARBONDALE, 1925 / GREEN OA VERONA, 1921 / GULPH MILLS GOLF CLUB, KING OF PRUSSIA, 1919 / KAHKWA CLUB, ERIE, 1915 / KENNETT SQUARE GOLF & COUNTRY CLUB, KENNETT SQUARE, 19 LEWISTOWN COUNTRY CLUB, LEWISTOWN, 1945 / LULU TEMPLE COUNTRY CLUB, NORTH HILLS, 1912 / OVERBROOK GOLF CLUB, PHILADELPHIA, 1922 / PHILADELPH CKC, PHILADELPHIA, 1914 / POCONO MANOR GOLF COURSE, WHITE HAVEN, 1919 / ROLLING ROCK CLUB, LIGONIER, 1916 / SCHUYLKILL COUNTRY CLUB, POTTSVIL 1945 / SILVERCREEK COUNTRY CLUB, HELLERTOWN, 1947 / ST. DAVIDS GOLF CLUB, WAYNE, 1927 / SUNNYBROOK COUNTRY CLUB, FLOURTOWN, 1921 / TORRESD FRANKFORD COUNTRY CLUB, PHILADELPHIA, 1919 / TUMBLEBROOK COUNTRY CLUB, COOPERS BROOK, 1931 / WHITEMARSH VALLEY COUNTRY CLUB, LAFAYETTE HI 1930 / COUNTRY CLUB OF YORK, YORK, 1927 / *RHODE ISLAND* / AGAWAM HUNT CLUB, RUMFORD, 1911 / METACOMET COUNTRY CLUB, EAST PROVIDENCE, 192 MISQUAMICUT CLUB, WESTERLY, 1923 / NEWPORT COUNTRY CLUB, NEWPORT, 1915 / POINT JUDITH COUNTRY CLUB, NARRAGANSETT, 1927 / RHODE ISLAND COUNT CLUB, WEST BARRINGTON, 1911 / SAKONNET GOLF CLUB, LITTLE COMPTON, 1921 / TRIGGS MEMORIAL GOLF CLUB, NORTH PROVIDENCE, 1930 / WANNAMOISETT COUNT CLUB, RUMFORD, 1914 / WARWICK COUNTRY CLUB, WARWICK NECK, 1924 / WINNAPAUG GOLF CLUB, WESTERLY, 1921 / *SOUTH CAROLINA* / CAMDEN COUNTRY CLU CAMDEN, 1939 / FORT MILL GOLF CLUB, FORT MILL, 1947 / LANCASTER GOLF CLUB, LANCASTER, 1935 / *TENNESSEE* / BELLE MEADE COUNTRY CLUB, NASHVILLE, 19 / BRAINERD GOLF & COUNTRY CLUB, CHATTANOOGA, 1925 / CHATTANOOGA COUNTRY CLUB, CHATTANOOGA, 1920 / CHEROKEE COUNTRY CLUB, KNOXVILLE, 19 HOLSTON HILLS COUNTRY CLUB, KNOXVILLE, 1928 / MEMPHIS COUNTRY CLUB, MEMPHIS, 1910 / RICHLAND COUNTRY CLUB, NASHVILLE, 1920 / RIDGEFIELDS COUNT CLUB, KINGSPORT, 1947 / TATE SPRINGS HOTEL & COUNTRY CLUB, BEAN STATION, 1924 / *TEXAS* / GALVESTON COUNTRY CLUB, GALVESTON, 1921 / RIVER OAKS COUN CLUB, HOUSTON, 1924 / SUNSET GROVE COUNTRY CLUB, ORANGE, 1923 / *VERMONT* / BURLINGTON COUNTRY CLUB, BURLINGTON, 1930 / WOODSTOCK COUNTRY CL WOODSTOCK, 1938 / *VIRGINIA* / BELMONT PARK, RICHMOND, 1940 / HAMPTON GOLF CLUB, HAMPTON, 1921 / THE HOMESTEAD HOTEL & GOLF CLUB, HOT SPRINGS, 1 / JEFFERSON-LAKESIDE COUNTRY CLUB, RICHMOND, 1921 / KINDERTON COUNTRY CLUB, CLARKSVILLE, 1947 / COUNTRY CLUB OF PETERSBURG, PETERSBURG, 192 SEWELLS PT. GOLF CLUB, NORFOLK, 1927 / COUNTRY CLUB OF VIRGINIA, RICHMOND, 1921 / WASHINGTON GOLF AND COUNTRY CLUB, ARLINGTON, 1915 / WESTWO GOLF CLUB, VIENNA, 1926 / WOODBURY FOREST GOLF CLUB, WOODBURY FOREST, 1910 / *WISCONSIN* / KENOSHA COUNTRY CLUB, KENOSHA, 1922 / OCONOMOW COUNTRY CLUB, OCONOMOWOC, 1915 / *CANADA* / ALGONQUIN HOTEL AND GOLF CLUB, ST. ANDREWS, NEW BRUNSWICK, 1927 / BANFF HOTEL GOLF CLUB, BANFF SPRIN 1912 / BRIGHTWOOD GOLF AND COUNTRY CLUB, DARTMOUTH, NOVA SCOTIA, 1934 / ESSEX GOLF AND COUNTRY CLUB, LASALLE, ONTARIO, 1929 / ELMHURST GOLF LIN WINNIPEG, MANITOBA, 1923 / LIVERPOOL GOLF CLUB, HUNTS POINT, NOVA SCOTIA, 1929 / PINE RIDGE COUNTRY CLUB, WINNIPEG, MANITOBA, 1919 / RIVERSIDE G AND COUNTRY CLUB, NEW BRUNSWICK, 1937 / ROSEDALE GOLF CLUB, TORONTO, ONTARIO, 1919 / ROSELAND GOLF AND COUNTRY CLUB, WINDSOR, ONTARIO, 192 ST. CHARLES COUNTRY CLUB, WINNIPEG, MANITOBA, 1920 / *CUBA* / COUNTRY CLUB OF HAVANA, HAVANA, 1911 / HAVANA BILTMORE GOLF CLUB, HAVANA, 19

GOLF, AS IT WAS MEANT TO BE PLAYED
A CELEBRATION OF DONALD ROSS'S VISION OF THE GAME

GOLF,

WAS ME

BE PL

A CELEBRATION O

VISION OF

BY MICHAE

PRINCIPAL PHOTOGRAPHY BY PAUL ROCHEL

UNIVERS

AS IT

F DONALD ROSS'S

ANT TO

THE GAME

AYED

.FAY WITH

AU AND ILLUSTRATIONS BY JOHN BURGOYNE

PUBLISHING

First published in the United States of America in 2000
by UNIVERSE PUBLISHING
A Division of Rizzoli International Publications, Inc.
300 Park Avenue South
New York, New York 10010

00 01 02 03 / 10 9 8 7 6 5 4 3 2 1

Library of Congress Cataloging-in-Publication Data

Fay, Michael
GOLF, AS IT WAS MEANT TO BE PLAYED:
A Celebration of Donald Ross's Vision of the Game / Michael Fay
p. cm.

ISBN 0-7893-0395-7 hardcover
ISBN 0-7893-0418-X deluxe limited edition
1. Golf. 2. Golf course design. 3. Landscape architecture.
I. Rocheleau, Paul. II. Gardner, A. Blake.

Edited by Richard Olsen

Design by Opto
Printed in England

IN EVERY LITERARY ATTEMPT THE AUTHOR IS NO MORE THAN A SPONGE SOAKING IN THE KNOWLEDGE AND KNOW-HOW OF HIS FRIENDS AND CONTEMPORARIES. THIS BOOK IS NO EXCEPTION.

I MUST FIRST GIVE PROPER CREDIT WHERE IT IS DUE. MY WIFE OF TWENTY-EIGHT YEARS, MONICA, WHO REMAINS AS PRETTY AS SHE WAS ON OUR WEDDING DAY, COULD WELL HAVE HAD ME COMMITTED NUMEROUS TIMES OVER THE YEARS. MONICA IS THE POSTER CHILD FOR THE GOLF WIDOWS ASSOCIATION AND YET REMAINS CHEERFUL AND UNDERSTANDING IN WATCHING MY RAMBLING QUEST IN THE WORLD OF GOLF. FOR HER PATIENCE AND ENCOURAGEMENT I DEDICATE THIS BOOK TO HER.

RICHARD OLSEN OF UNIVERSE PUBLISHING IS MY EDITOR; A FINE FELLOW, A TERRIBLE GOLFER, YET A GREAT MOTIVATOR AND AN ORGANIZER PAR EXCELLENCE. WITHOUT RICHARD, THIS BOOK WOULD BE A COLLECTION OF SCATOLOGICAL PAGES OF SCRIBBLE OCCUPYING SPACE ON MY DESK. ALSO AT UNIVERSE, I EXTEND MANY THANKS TO MANAGING EDITOR BONNIE ELDON, PRODUCTION MANAGER BELINDA HELLINGER, AND PUBLISHER CHARLES MIERS, WHOSE VISION AND ENTHUSIASM HELPED CARRY THIS BOOK TO ITS COMPLETION.

FOR THE BOOK'S EXCEPTIONAL DESIGN, I THANK JOHN KLOTNIA AND BRAD SIMON OF OPTO DESIGN IN NEW YORK.

MANY TIMES I AVAILED MYSELF OF THE INVALUABLE ASSISTANCE OF KHRISTINE JANUZIK OF THE TUFTS ARCHIVES (OF THE GIVEN MEMORIAL LIBRARY) IN PINEHURST. THANKS, KHRIS.

THANKS TO MY FRIENDS AT THE COURSES FEATURED IN THE BOOK: JOHN TRICKETT AND PGA PROFESSIONAL JIM MASSARIO OF ARONOMINK, WITH WHOM I HAVE PLAYED THIS REMARKABLE GOLF COURSE; AT SCIOTO, WAYNE ASHBY, MY FRIEND, MENTOR, AND ONE OF THE GREATEST ASSETS IN GOLF; AT WANNAMOISETT, MICHAEL BURKE, DENNIS GLASS, AND THE OTHERS WITH WHOM I HAVE ENJOYED WALKING THESE HALLOWED GROUNDS; AT BRAE BURN, THE BOYS IN THE PRO SHOP AND FRANK MORGAN, WHO FIRST SHOWED ME THIS WONDERFUL COURSE; THE STAFF AT PINEHURST RESORT AND COUNTRY CLUB; JACK BROADBRIDGE, JEFF WITHERWAX, AND TOM GLEETON AT THE COUNTRY CLUB OF WATERBURY; MIKE MILLER, JOHN WYLIE, AND ESPECIALLY JOHN STILES FOR THEIR INPUT ON THE SEVENTH AT HOLSTON HILLS; DR. BILL ROBISCHON, BILL REEVES, AND BILL THANEY, THREE OF THE MOST DEDICATED SUPPORTERS OF GOLF AND DEFENDERS OF THE TRADITIONS OF OAK HILL COUNTRY CLUB; EDMUND MAURO OF POINT JUDITH, FOUNDER AND CHIEF EXECUTIVE OF THE BUTTONHOLE PROJECT IN RHODE ISLAND AND A GUY WHO IS GIVING BACK TO GOLF EVERYTHING IT HAS PROVIDED HIM AND MORE; TOM SMACK, A PROFESSIONAL'S PROFESSIONAL, THE SAVIOR OF THE ROSS COURSE AT THE SAGAMORE, AND SOMEONE WHO WILL DO ANYTHING TO FURTHER THE GAME OF GOLF; GEORGE BURKE OF BEVERLY, MASSACHUSETTS, FOR HIS WONDERFUL INSIGHTS TO EVERY NOOK AND CRANNY AT THE ELEVENTH AT ESSEX COUNTY CLUB; TOM CASTRONOVO OF THE PLAINFIELD COUNTRY CLUB, WITH WHOM I TOURED THIS COURSE IN THE PAST YEAR AND WHO IS TRULY DEDICATED TO THE PRESERVATION OF THE ROSS FEATURES THERE; TERRY O'MALLEY, GEORGE BURKE, AND A CAST OF HUNDREDS AT THE SALEM COUNTRY CLUB (MY FAVORITE GOLF COURSE IN NEW ENGLAND AND ONE OF THE BEST-PRESERVED ROSS COURSES ANYWHERE); ED TWOHIG, THE PROFESSIONAL AT THE ORCHARDS, FOR HIS LONG-TERM HOSPITALITY AND VALUABLE INSIGHTS; MY GOOD FRIEND MEL FULTZ, CLUB HISTORIAN OF THE INVERNESS CLUB IN TOLEDO; PAUL MERSEREAU, RICHARD GORDON, AND TRACEY STANGLE OF THE HARTFORD GOLF CLUB; JOHN WHEALON AND PAUL LAZAR, WHO HAVE BEEN ALLIES AND WONDERFUL HOSTS AT THE WORCESTER COUNTRY CLUB.

I OWE A LOT TO MANY PEOPLE AT WAMPANOAG COUNTRY CLUB, MY HOME-AWAY-FROM-HOME FOR SOME FORTY YEARS. THERE ARE NONE, HOWEVER, TO WHOM I OWE MORE THAN MY FATHER, JOHN E. FAY, WHO, MANY, MANY YEARS AGO, INTRODUCED ME TO THE GAME OF GOLF AND WAMPANOAG. TO ALL OF MY FRIENDS AT WAMP, I SAY HI!

LEST I FORGET, THE CREW AT PINE NEEDLES AND MID PINES: KELLY MILLER, HELEN DOWNIE, CLUB PROFESSIONAL CHIP KING, BARRETT WALKER, HOLLY BELL, AND ALL OF THE OTHERS WHO MAKE THIS OPERATION ONE OF THE GREATEST EXPERIENCES IN GOLF. AND A VERY SPECIAL THANKS TO THEIR LEADER AND THE FIRST LADY OF GOLF, PEGGY KIRK BELL.

TO THE SEVENTEEN-HUNDRED MEMBERS OF THE DONALD ROSS SOCIETY WHO HAVE CONTRIBUTED IN ONE WAY OR ANOTHER TO THIS EFFORT—WHETHER THEY KNOW IT OR NOT—I THANK YOU ALL.

ACKNOWLEDGMENTS

DONALD ROSS AND I have a rather long history. I grew up in Findlay, Ohio, and as a girl had the privilege of playing fairly often the Inverness Course in nearby Toledo. I always loved playing Inverness, though I did not know that it was a Ross course.

In the 1940s, while playing golf for Rollins College in Florida, I traveled to Pinehurst for the first time, with the intention of competing in the Women's North and South Amateur. I presented myself at the front desk of the Pinehurst Country Club pro shop and announced to the person on duty that I was there to pay my entry fee. Much to my embarrassment, the clerk informed me that the Women's North and South Amateur is an invitational event. As I was doing my best to crawl under a rug, a gentleman said very quickly that I should stay where I was for a

few minutes. About two minutes later, the gentleman, Mr. Richard Tufts, emerged from behind the counter with a hastily penned invitation.

For this gesture, I would always love the Sandhills, but there are many other great memories from the early days in Pinehurst. In the late 1940s I met Donald Ross, and in 1949, I won the Women's North and South Amateur Championship. In 1952, my husband, Warren "Bullet" Bell, and I spent more money than either of us ever imagined possible—fifty-thousand dollars to buy the Pine Needles Golf Club. In the late 1950s, I started the Golf School at Pine Needles and, after Bullet and I built the Lodge, initiated the club's first Golfari. The school and the Golfaris continue to this day.

As years went by, my relationship with the work of Donald Ross grew stronger. In the mid-1990s, I joined a syndicate to buy the Mid Pines Hotel and Golf Club—the club adjacent to Pine Needles. The deal was a success. Today, our family runs Pine Needles and Mid Pines. And when I'm not on one of our courses, I play my golf at another Donald Ross creation, the Seminole Country Club in North Palm Beach, Florida.

I have a very strong affinity for the work of Donald Ross and believe in the importance of preserving it. My good friend Peter Dye was once approached to change the eighteenth green at the Inverness Club to prepare for a major championship. After a great deal of thought, Peter told the "powers that be" that he would accommodate their request for the tournament but only on the condition that he would be allowed to change it back right after the event. This is the way I feel about Donald Ross-designed courses. They are time pieces that are as relevant today as when they were built.

I applaud the Donald Ross Society and Michael Fay for the work done in this area. And I hope you enjoy the book.

Peggy Kirk Bell

Peggy Kirk Bell

DONALD ROSS

IF EVER THERE was a man at the right place at the right time to pursue his passion and gain fame it was Donald J. Ross.

His story began in Dornoch, north of the Highlands, fast to the sea on the east coast of Scotland, 700 miles from the Arctic Circle. One might think this very unlikely geography to spawn a man so closely identified with the game of golf, until it is remembered that the Gulf Stream wanders across the Atlantic, touches the west coast of Ireland, heads north and east and thence down the east coast of Scotland. Luckily for Ross and the game of golf, the Gulf Stream winds past Dornoch, and brings with it moderate temperatures and pleasant atmosphere.

Ross was born in 1872 to a family of modest means in Dornoch. Ross's father, Mundo, was

ALWAYS DAPPERLY ATTIRED—ROSS AT THE TURN OF THE CENTURY. PHOTO COURTESY OF THE TUFTS ARCHIVES (OF THE GIVEN MEMORIAL LIBRARY)

a stonemason. Ross, in his mid-teens, became a carpenter's apprentice. Fortune stepped in at this point of his life. Ross as a youth was an accomplished golfer on the links at Dornoch and came under the eye of Donald Sutherland, the club secretary. Sutherland took the young Ross under his wing and began to groom him for the role of club professional and greenkeeper at the links.

GENERAL PLAN OF PINEHURST.

ABOVE: THE MASSACHUSETTS FIRM OF OLMSTED. OLMSTED & ELLIOT DRAFTED THE GENERAL PLAN OF PINEHURST. POSITIONED AT THE HEART OF THE VILLAGE IS THE HOLLY INN, STILL ONE OF THE MOST POPULAR DESTINATIONS IN TOWN FOR THE VISITING GOLFER. *OPPOSITE PAGE:* ROSS ATTEMPTED DIFFERENT SHOTS WHILE LAYING OUT HIS COURSES, AS EXAMPLE, SEEN HERE ON THE UNCOMPLETED #4 COURSE AT PINEHURST.

He was sent to St. Andrews—the golf capital of the world—to learn from the most highly recognized professional of the time, Old Tom Morris. Morris was not only a champion golfer (he won the British Open championship three of the first four years the tournament was played), he was also greatly sought for his efforts in golf course design. Morris traveled all over the British Isles in the latter part of the nineteenth century designing courses that are revered to this day. In Ireland, he created Lahinch in the southwest and Royal County Down in the northeast; in England he built a number of courses, the most famous of which is Royal North Devon. In Scotland, his work can be seen at St. Andrews, where he remodeled the Old Course and created the New Course; at Carnoustie, where he added six holes; and at many links courses, including Moray Golf Club, Crail, and Tain.

While at St. Andrews, Ross learned the intricacies of the professional's duties. In addition, he worked in the famous clubmaker David Forgan's shop, building golf clubs and molding golf balls

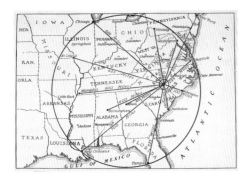

from gutta percha. In 1893 he returned to Dornoch to take on the responsibilities of his new appointment of club professional and greenkeeper. By 1899, Ross was well-established as the man in charge at the links of Dornoch; his future seemed modest but secure.

Soon thereafter, Professor Robert Willson met young Ross on a holiday in Scotland and was quite taken by the young professional's talents. Willson impressed upon Ross the limitless future of golf in the United States. Golf had only been played for a decade or so in the U.S. but had become very popular, especially among the wealthy. The locals in Dornoch were quite shocked when Ross forsook his secure paying position (300 pounds annually) to emigrate to the United States.

Ross arrived in 1899, where he assumed the position of club professional and greenkeeper at the Oakley Country Club in Watertown, Massachusetts. He found it an optimum time to come to the United States with knowledge and

IN THE MID-NINETEENTH CENTURY THE ORIGINAL GOLF BALL, THE FEATHERIE (MADE FROM ENCASED DAMPENED GOOSE FEATHERS), WAS REPLACED BY THE GUTTA PERCHA BALL. GUTTA PERCHA IS A SUBSTANCE THAT IS GATHERED FROM A TREE NATIVE TO THE FAR EAST. WHEN GUTTA PERCHA IS HEATED, IT CAN BE MOLDED; AS IT COOLS, IT HARDENS. GOLF BALLS WERE MANUFACTURED FROM MOLDED GUTTA PERCHA UNTIL COBURN HASKELL INVENTED THE WOUND BALL AT THE TURN OF THE CENTURY. KNOWN AS THE HASKELL WOUND BALL, IT WAS NOT ONLY CHEAPER TO MANUFACTURE BUT COULD FLY SIGNIFICANTLY FARTHER AND ACTUALLY STOP QUITE ABRUPTLY IF HIT WITH THE RIGHT TOUCH. USED BY THE WINNER OF THE BRITISH OPEN CHAMPIONSHIP OF 1902, THE HASKELL WOUND BALL QUICKLY BECAME THE STANDARD AND REMAINED AS SUCH UNTIL THE SPALDING COMPANY INTRODUCED IN 1968 ITS REVOLUTIONARY TWO-PIECE BALL CALLED TOP FLITE.

know-how in the game of golf. There were very few golf courses and those that existed were to be made obsolete within five years upon the invention of the Haskell wound ball (the existing golf courses had been built to accommodate the gutta percha ball, which did not travel as high or as far as its new wound successor).

One of Ross's earliest duties at Oakley was to redesign the rudimentary course, which immediately led to his being called upon to design other courses in the local area. At Oakley, Ross met James Tufts of the American Soda Fountain Company. Tufts had recently bought a large tract of land in the sandhills of south central North Carolina to establish a winter resort away from the

ABOVE: AN EARLY ADVERTISEMENT FOR JAMES W. TUFTS'S PINEHURST. NOTE THE NUMBER OF GUESTS PINEHURST COULD ACCOMMODATE IN THOSE DAYS. PHOTO COURTESY OF THE TUFTS ARCHIVES (OF THE GIVEN MEMORIAL LIBRARY)

harsh weather of New England. This rural tract, accessible only by rail, was known as Pinehurst.

Tufts convinced Ross to accompany him on a trip south, in 1900, to become the director of golf at the Pinehurst Resort, a title he would retain until his death. This journey established a precedent Ross would follow the remainder of his days: He would work in New England in the summers and in North Carolina in the winters.

Ross designed and redesigned a number of courses in the first decade of the twentieth century, yet he still took his responsibilities as club professional and greenkeeper seriously. He competed in a number of tournaments, winning the Massachusetts Open and the North and South Open, and finished well in a number of U.S. Opens.

In 1909, Ross was hired as club professional by Essex County Club in Manchester, Massachusetts, a position he held until 1913. Overwhelmed with the demand for his design work,

DONALD ROSS

23

he chose to leave Essex to focus full-time on course architecture. By 1916, Donald J. Ross Associates was established, with J.B. McGovern of Wynnewood, Pennsylvania, and Walter Hatch of Amherst, Massachusetts, serving as his engineers and Walter Irving Johnston as draftsman and technician.

During the first three decades of the twentieth century, Ross's practice was in such great demand that he employed some 30 building crews and 2,500 men. They were responsible for the design and construction of more than 380 courses. One of the most fascinating aspects of Ross's design business was that the work came to him without significant solicitation. A review of his records reveals that in only two instances did Ross solicit work. One of those projects was to become one of his most famous works, the Seminole Golf Club in North Palm Beach, Florida. The other solicitation was unsuccessful and became his greatest disappointment, as he lost out to Alister Mackenzie in vying for the project at the Augusta National Golf Club in Augusta, Georgia.

Nevertheless, Ross's courses were immediately embraced and became the favorite sites of professional and amateur tournaments. From 1919 to 1930, the national open was played on no fewer than seven different Ross designs. Though golf in America struggled during the incredibly difficult times of the Great Depression, this trend endured for another 70 years of championship play.

Throughout the 1990s, every year Ross-designed courses have been the sites of different

OPPOSITE PAGE: BUILT IN 1925, ROSS OCCUPIED THIS HOUSE UNTIL HIS DEATH IN 1948. THE HOUSE HAS BEEN TOTALLY RESTORED BY JO AND WAYNE ASHBY.

U.S.G.A. Championships, ranging from the Girls' Junior to the U.S. Open. In 1998 alone, the USGA Senior Amateur was held at Skokie

Country Club in Glencoe, Illinois, the U.S. Women's Amateur at OPPOSITE PAGE: BEN HOGAN, WHO WON HIS FIRST PROFES-
SIONAL TOURNAMENT AT PINEHURST, PLAYS FROM A BUNKER. Barton Hills Country Club in Ann Arbor, Michigan, and the U.S. Amateur at the East Course at Oak Hill Country Club in Rochester, New York. In 1999, the U.S. Junior Amateur was held at the Country Club of York in York, Pennsylvania, the U.S. Women's Amateur was played at the Biltmore Forest Country Club in Asheville, North Carolina, and the U.S. Open was contested at the hallowed grounds of Course Number 2 at the Pinehurst Resort and Country Club in Pinehurst, North Carolina. The twentieth century has seen more than 120 USGA Championships played on Ross-designed courses.

By the time of Ross's death of a heart attack in 1948 at the age of 75, at least 413 courses had been designed by his firm. Today, one can experience Ross's work and his impact on the game by visiting any of the courses touched by his talents, in 30 states across America, and in Canada, Nova Scotia, and Cuba.

THE DESIGN PHILOSOPHY OF DONALD ROSS

MANY INTERPRET Donald Ross's design philosophy as quite intricate. Unlike the work of most of his peers, Ross's hole designs did not repeat from course to course. Each was original and designed specifically for the landscape on which it was built. Laying out the golf course was a practical matter for Ross; his methods were simple but artful. He wanted to return to the clubhouse in

two loops if possible and at the same time take advantage of existing plateaus and hills. For Ross it was imperative to incorporate the high ground, as this was the most effective natural drainage system he could employ.

Ross designs were sensible in their creation. For Ross believed that golf should be a pleasure and not a penance. With this in mind, he designed courses that were playable by nearly every level of golfer. He did not create excessive hazards to punish the errant shot. Believing that a vertical hazard was simply unfair, Ross was sensitive to the positioning of trees in the fairway. Furthermore, if possible, he avoided the use of water hazards. When faced with no other choice but to incorporate a stream or a pond, he tried to use the hazard in such a way that it did not become the focal point of the hole. He designed and built sensible bunkers—ones that were strategically placed, yet not penal in nature. If a player found himself in a bunker 160 yards from the green, recovery was usually within reach as the bunker was constructed to allow for a well-struck shot to reach its target. Certainly, some of the courses he created were a great deal more difficult than the average. Many of these more challenging courses were likely built specifically for championship play.

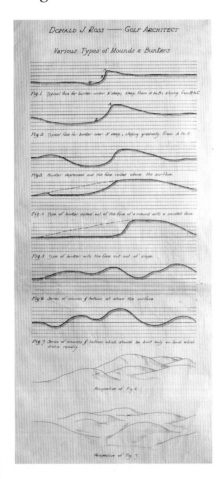

Continuity was another important principle of Ross's design philosophy. His courses were meant to flow without interruption. An unbroken reverie was established from the first tee to the eighteenth green. He wanted the player to feel that the holes occurred naturally, without the meddling of the architect. Changes in elevation were handled in an unconventional manner. While many of his peers dealt with elevation suddenly and abruptly, Ross's approach was far more subtle. He would walk the player up the hill gradually, almost imperceptibly. An elevation change of three hundred feet could take as many as five or six holes. Typically, Ross would elevate the tees on these holes to further assuage the difficulty of the elevation change. Ross also believed that golf is meant to be played close to the ground, and he accommodated the player who hit shots low into the greens by creating openings in front of most of them. This was very much in the tradition of golf in Scotland where extreme winds frequently force players to play low for greater control.

Another significant aspect of the continuity found on Ross courses is the absence of drastic directional changes. Few of his courses were built with the endless back-and-forth seen in the work of many other designers. Rather, he gently turned the player in differing directions. This tactic afforded Ross the ability to incorporate into the game prevailing winds, either to aid or to hinder depending on his intent. Many of Ross's finishing holes are long par fours. It was his belief that the most dramatic shot in the game was a well-struck long iron. In fact, he intention-

ally designed many finishing par fours to be played into a prevailing wind.

Ross often built his greens with a number of approaches, yet only one best line of play. By design, his greens accept and reward well-struck and well-placed shots and often repel the errant missile. A player might be able to land a less than competent shot on the green, but he would have great difficulty in either keeping it there or two-putting for par. Ross designed larger, less-undulating greens for the long par three and par four holes, and smaller targets for the par five holes and the shorter threes and fours.

Practicality may have been the most important principle of Ross's design philosophy. It must be remembered that in Ross's day there were severe limitations on the moving of dirt. Most of this work was accomplished by the use of horse- or ox-drawn carts. Fortunately for Ross, most of the sites on which he built courses were already cleared of most vegetation, trees, and rocks. In final preparation to build, Ross's team would gather the remaining tree stumps and boulders in strategic places, pile them up, and cover them with dirt. Those mounds can be found today on many of Ross's golf courses.

Because of his background as a greenkeeper, Ross was more attentive to drainage problems than the average architect. He was very careful in the placement of bunkers so that they could be constructed with proper drainage. Fairways, greens, tees, and bunkers were positioned in a manner to best utilize natural slopes that would carry the water to ponds and streams. In some instances, where the land was extraordinarily flat, Ross dug drainage canals around the property and then built the course so that the contoured slopes would carry off the water.

To this day, some of Ross's simple but effective problem-solving techniques are still in use at courses across America.

ON THE RELEVANCE OF

CLASSIC DESIGN

THROUGHOUT THE 1940s, 1950s, and 1960s, the golf ball and the golf club were constantly improved, but the improvements were not revolutionary. For instance, in the early 1960s, a golfer could purchase a sleeve of balls, take them out of their wrapping, and roll them on a flat, hard surface. If he were lucky, perhaps one of the balls would be perfectly round. Even at this point, the covers of the balls were inordinately soft and could be cut rather easily.

The more significant changes of this period occurred in the area of course maintenance. In the 1950s, many clubs began to introduce watering systems for their fairways. Up to this point, fairways had been hard and fast, usually covered with brown, burned-out turf by mid-summer. Before the sprinkler systems, the only parts of the course that were eternally green were the greens and tees.

The introduction of watered fairways changed the nature of golf to some degree by raising the plane. It became more important to move the ball in the air rather than on the ground. Lush

ACTIVITIES AT MANIAC HILL IN PINEHURST,
THE FIRST REAL PRACTICE RANGE, ANYWHERE.
DESIGNED BY DONALD ROSS. PHOTO COURTESY
OF THE TUFTS ARCHIVES (OF THE GIVEN MEMORI-
AL LIBRARY)

fairways did not allow for the roll that had been enjoyed in the past and, as a consequence, golf courses actually began to play longer.

By the end of the 1970s a number of additional elements changed in the game of golf. The ball was made hotter and more standardized. It was now the exception when a new ball was found to be out of round. This standardization of the ball helped it to fly farther and more consistently. Also, new materials were employed in the construction of golf clubs. The vaunted one-piece persimmon wood had transformed into the new oxymoronic metal wood. Perimeter weighting replaced the straight and unforgiving shape of iron clubs.

While this was going on in the equipment industry, the agronomists were busily at work. New strains of grass were discovered and new equipment was developed for tending to the courses. Sprinkler systems were expanded into many new areas, including the rough. Greens could be cut to a much lower tolerance without fear of loss. Putting became a much larger part of the protection of par.

With all this give-and-take of equipment for playing and equipment for maintenance, what is the overall effect on the courses built in the first quarter of the century? Do classically designed golf courses truly lack the elements necessary to protect par from the modern equipment of today?

Mostly it is a wash. The average player does not score any better on the courses of the 1920s than did the player of that era. The new playing equipment seems to have been offset by the advances in course maintenance. If there is any real difference for the average player, it is that the shorter par five holes have become reachable, making them more like a par four-and-one-half.

Today, this is not the case in the professional game. Distance has been overcome through improvements in the clubs and balls. Senior tour players are the first to admit they hit the ball farther today with their graphite-shafted titanium-headed clubs than they ever did in their prime.

To the vast majority of touring players there is no such animal as a par five, there are only long par fours. Today, drives in excess of three hundred and twenty yards are not uncommon. Today's touring professional is better conditioned, better taught, and better equipped. The golf courses of yesteryear are no longer the challenge that they were to these players. The only aspect of the old game that has remained difficult through the years is

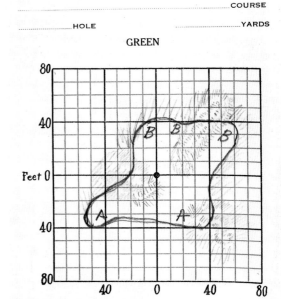

NOTES

.... COURSE ....

.... HOLE .... YARDS

GREEN

RIGHT: HOW TO ADDRESS DRAINAGE PROBLEMS WAS A CONSTANT BATTLE FOR ARCHITECTS OF ROSS'S ERA. SOMEHOW, ROSS ALWAYS SEEMED TO WIN. THIS EARLY DRAWING BY ROSS IS ACCOMPANIED BY SPECIFIC INSTRUCTIONS ON THE TOPIC. PHOTO COURTESY OF THE TUFTS ARCHIVES (OF THE GIVEN MEMORIAL LIBRARY)

the one practiced with the putter. Green speeds today are vastly accelerated over the green speeds of yesteryear. This puts a great deal more emphasis on the positioning of the ball on the green and the ability to putt.

Ross must have seen this coming. Unlike the greens of many other designers, Ross built a high degree of difficulty into his surfaces. Nearly all of the greens he designed slope fairly dramatically from back to front, and less dramatically to one side or the other. His greens contain subtle contours to bedevil the player. From the beginning, Ross defended par at the green, and in so doing, made his courses for the ages.

HOW TO SPOT A CLASSIC COURSE

THERE ARE THREE different significant periods in golf course architecture in the history of the game in the United States. They are the Classic Era, the Mechanical Era, and the Modern Era.

The Modern Era work is that which we see most of today on heralded new golf courses. The Modern Era game is most often played in the air. Typically there is an inordinate amount of water hazards, and peninsular and island greens. Invariably, the greens are unapproachable on the ground. They tend to be raised significantly above the fairways and are more often than not fronted by bunkering that disallows the use of any pitch and run options. Modern Era courses tend to be aesthetically perfect and, more

OPPOSITE PAGE: CLUB SELECTION WAS NEVER TAKEN LIGHTLY BY ROSS. HERE, PREPARING TO TEE OFF AT PINEHURST, ROSS REACHES FOR THE MAGIC NUMBER. PHOTO COURTESY OF THE TUFTS ARCHIVES (OF THE GIVEN MEMORIAL LIBRARY)

LOOKING FROM THE TEE AT INTERLACHEN NO. 18,
BUILT IN 1919, YOU CAN SEE THE ORIGINAL LAY
OF THE LAND INCORPORATED INTO A GOLF HOLE.

often than not, difficult for the less than talented player. Shots hit from fairways are an exercise in height and the gauging of distance and wind conditions. The ability to massage the golf ball with the proper amount of backspin is crucial. Bunkers on modern courses tend to be more of an integral part of the overall landscape than strategic playable hazards. I have seen bunkers so severely sloped that the only egress is to stand with one's back to the hole and hit the ball over one's shoulder. Many, however pretty and well placed from an aesthetic point of view, in my opinion, are without golf value.

The American Society of Golf Course Architects held its first annual meeting in Pinehurst on Dec. 5, 1947. Shown at that meeting (l. to r.) are: William P. Bell, Pasadena, Calif.; Robert White, Myrtle Beach, S.C.; W. B. Langford, Chicago, Ill.; Honorary President Donald J. Ross, Pinehurst, N.C.; President Robert Bruce Harris, Chicago, Ill.; Vice President Stanley Thompson, Toronto, Canada; William F. Gordon, Doylestown, Pa.; Secretary-Treasurer Robert Trent Jones, Montclair, N.J.; William Diddel, Carmel, Ind.; and J. B. McGovern, Wynnewood, Pa. Three of the original 13 charter members were not able to attend the first Pinehurst meeting: Perry Maxwell, Ardmore, Okla.; Jack Daray, Chicago, Ill.; and Robert F. "Red" Lawrence, Boca Raton, Fla. Donald Ross and his partner, J. B. McGovern, were the Society's hosts at the meeting. Today the Society's highest honor--the Donald Ross Award--is presented annually to a person who has made a significant contribution to the

AMERICAN SOCIETY OF GOLF COURSE ARCHITECTS INAUGUR-
AL MEETING. ROSS WAS THE FOUNDER AND FIRST PRESIDENT
IN 1947.

The Mechanical Era is the period from World War II through 1970, one that was dominated by the work of Robert Trent Jones. I refer to these years as the Mechanical Era for two reasons. Firstly, man, with the aid of a small amount of machinery, had primarily executed the construction of golf courses prior to this period. By this time, the golf course architect had bulldozers, landmovers, and many other mechanized implements at his disposal. Secondly, golf course architects of this era tended to manufacture plans rather than design golf courses. By this I mean that the holes were created in the drawing room and then painted on the landscape with the help of the machinery. The Mechanical Era lengthened golf courses, employed a greater amount of landscape architecture and defended par with length and hazards. Bunkers were large, deep, and beveled. The design of greens tended to be somewhat unimaginative and more about easy maintenance than true golf values.

The Classic Era featured courses that were designed either to be strategic or penal. The strategic course would often feature hazards that imposed a half-shot penalty (e.g., partially blocked egress after a missed shot, bunkers positioned to catch errant shots where a player could only save par with a truly great recovery shot). Penal courses provided tees, fairways, and greens.

The classic course was not groomed; its tees, fairways, and greens were cut and eminently playable. The rest of the course was nature. Natural grasses and weeds were allowed to flourish in the out-of-play area. Left unkempt were any natural formations such as hills, plateaus, rills, and ponds. They may or may not have been incorporated into the scheme of the design, but one way or another they were left unchanged.

The classic course, particularly from a shaping point of view, offers the player the most interesting greens, forcing the player to position the approach shot in such a way that drastic downhill and sidehill putts can be avoided.

To recognize a classic course is simple. If you play the first six holes and hit them all in regulation and walk to the seventh tee five over par, you have just encountered a classic course—the work of one of the masters of golf architecture.

THE HOLES CHOSEN for this book are from courses designed by Donald Ross between the years 1907 and 1936. In compiling the holes into one course the author has attempted to choose holes that have received minimal alterations over the years. In some instances, like the fifth hole at Pinehurst Course Number 2, the hole is essentially the same as when it was designed in 1936. The only modification has been the occasional movement of the tee to elongate the hole. Other holes such as No. 3 at Wannamoisett, No. 13 at Salem, No. 7 at Holston Hills, and No. 12 at Plainfield Country Club have been either preserved over the years or restored to their original design based on the drawings left by Ross.

Many of the other holes are very much the way they were originally designed, but have been altered by green chairmen, green committees, or latter-day architects. While they are not purely the work of Ross, these holes are a tribute to his talent and still contain enough of the original Ross genius to be showcased in this volume.

Selecting the holes for this book was very difficult. While there is a very large body of work that is attributed to Ross, only eighteen holes could be chosen. The author apologizes to his many friends at the Ross courses that are not included here.

ABOVE: A LETTER FROM ROSS TO JAMES TUFTS. PHOTO COURTESY OF THE TUFTS ARCHIVES (OF THE GIVEN MEMORIAL LIBRARY)

OPPOSITE PAGE: THE "ROSS ROOM" AT THE DORNOCH COTTAGE, VILLAGE OF PINEHURST, 1999.

A GOLFER'S STROLL THR

OUGH 18 PERFECT HOLES

A STERN
HANDSHAKE ARONIMINK

NUMBER

"Hole Number 1 is very deceptive. Many players assume that, because the view of the hole from the elevated tee is quite clear, it's an easy start. What they soon discover is that Ross had the exact opposite in mind when he laid it out." Rick Holanda, Course Superintendent, Aronimink

NUMBER
1

NEWTOWN SQUARE, PENNSYLVANIA • 1928
420 YARDS • PAR 4

IN HIS BOOK *Golf Has Never Failed Me*, Donald Ross describes an ideal first hole as a handshake to prepare the golfer for what is to come. At the Aronimink Golf Club in Newtown Square, Pennsylvania, the handshake is a bit more firm than the player is expecting. Frankly, the opener at Aronimink is downright scary.

The view from the first tee at Aronimink is not for the weak of heart. The fairway, which is rather generous, is guarded left and right by the forest primeval. The one feature that is sure to catch the player's eye is the yawning bunker that emanates from the rough on the right about 235

STATELY IS NOT OFTEN an understatement. As a description of the Aronimink Country Club clubhouse and grounds, it is inadequate. The sturdy Georgian clubhouse, surrounded by the magnificently manicured grounds, conjures up at the very least the word elegant and more probably princely. This Philadelphia mainline (Newtown Square) club is as imposing as any in the folio of Ross. Upon approaching the property, a visitor cannot help but feel the air of total competence that pervades the territory. This is not only true of the initial sighting of the driveway and building, but the golf course as well.

STANDING ON THE TEE AND LOOKING DOWN
THE LANE WHILE THE BUNKERS BEG FOR
YOUR ATTENTION.

THE PLAYER EYEING THE GREEN FROM BEHIND
THIS BUNKER BETTER BE ON GOOD TERMS WITH
HIS MIDDLE IRONS.

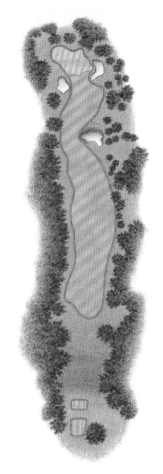

yards from the tee and covers fully one-third of the fairway. The player is immediately aware that this is not the place to be. The opening drive in any round is important, especially so at Aronimink. The hole is about 420 yards long, plays down to a hollow and then back up gradually to the green. To have any hope for a successful second shot, the player must hit the ball 240-plus yards. This automatically brings the right fairway bunker into play. Standing on the tee, the player must take his aim, relax, and trust his swing. A hook or slice and the golfer is looking at bogey or worse.

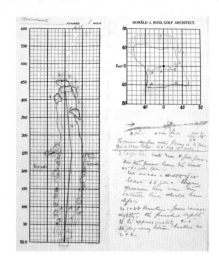

LEFT: NUMBER 1, AS ILLUSTRATED BY JOHN BURGOYNE, 2000. *ABOVE:* DETAIL OF NO. 1, ILLUSTRATED AND WITH SPECIFIC INSTRUCTIONS BY ROSS, 1927. PHOTO COURTESY OF THE TUFTS ARCHIVES (OF THE GIVEN MEMORIAL LIBRARY).

If the drive is well struck, the second is difficult but not overwhelming. A middle iron—played well from the fairway—should find the enormous green, which is elliptically shaped and slopes significantly from back to front. Although the green's surface is unseen from the fairway, there are no hidden tricks.

OPPOSITE PAGE: ON THE GREEN AND LOOKING FOR AN EARLY BIRDIE AT ARONIMINK.

Par is a really good number on the first at Aronimink. Birdie is a triumph. But beware, this is a handshake that can crush your knuckles.

WHERE JONES
MEETS NICKLAUS SCIOTO

NUMBER
2

"It is the best conditioned course I've ever played on, and by far the best test we've
played since I've been on the Senior Tour. I wish we'd play
more courses like this." Gary Player, before the 1986 Senior Open at Scioto

NUMBER
2

COLUMBUS, OHIO • 1916
459 YARDS • PAR 4

SCIOTO COULD BE DESCRIBED as the perfect place to learn the championship game. It requires the ability to hit the golf ball long and straight off the tee, expertise with all clubs to reach the greens, and a deft touch on or around the putting surfaces. A round at Scioto will require the use of all 14 clubs. Without sufficient forethought and expertise in implementation, there can be no successful shots hit at Scioto. This course will absolutely wring the neck of the thoughtless or careless player. Like Ross, it will suffer no fools.

The drive must be long and straight. Anything out of the fairway will make five a good score.

COLUMBUS, OHIO, MAY NOT BE the best city in the United States for golf, but it is certainly in the running. Within a very small radius, the golfer can find Alister Mackenzie's Scarlet Course at Ohio State, Pete Dye's masterpiece, The Golf Club, Jack Nicklaus and Desmond Muirhead's Muirfield Village, Tom Weiskopf and Jay Morrish's Double Eagle Club, and last but not least a 1916 Donald Ross design, Scioto Country Club. Scioto Country Club is a very special venue. It has hosted major championships, including the U.S. Open, the Ryder Cup, and the PGA Championship. It has been the site of endless Ohio State golf events and city championships. Most of all, it was the home of Jack W. Nicklaus.

THIS BEAUTIFUL VIEW FROM THE TEE REVEALS
A SMALL WATER HAZARD AND A FEW POTENTIALLY
PROBLEMATIC BUNKERS.

WHEN PLAYING THIS HOLE—UNLESS YOU'RE JACK
NICKLAUS—YOU'LL OCCASIONALLY LEAVE IT HAV-
ING DONE A BIT OF RAKING.

NICKLAUS LEARNED THE GAME OF GOLF AT SCIOTO COUNTRY CLUB UNDER THE WATCHFUL EYE OF JACK GROUT, THE THEN-HEAD PROFESSIONAL. AS A YOUTH, NICKLAUS WAS A DENIZEN OF SCIOTO, THERE EARLY EVERY DAY TAKING LESSONS, BEATING BALLS, AND PLAYING. HE WOULD PRACTICE ENDLESS HOURS ON THE PUTTING GREEN, OFTENTIMES INTO AND BEYOND THE DUSK. GROUT SAID MANY TIMES THAT NICKLAUS WAS THE PERFECT STUDENT, WILLING TO PUT IN ALL THE EFFORT NECESSARY TO REACH SUCCESS. THE EVOLUTION OF THE GAME OF NICKLAUS IS CHRONICLED IN PHOTOGRAPHS THAT ADORN THE WALLS OF THE CLUBHOUSE.

THERE IS ONE OTHER VERY SIGNIFICANT PICTURE ON THE WALL AT SCIOTO, ONE THAT CANNOT BE OVERLOOKED, ONE THAT PROBABLY INSPIRED THE SUBJECT OF THE OTHER PHOTOS. THAT PICTURE IS OF ROBERT TYRE JONES II HOLDING THE U.S. OPEN TROPHY FOR HIS WIN IN THE 1926 OPEN AT SCIOTO. ONE CAN EASILY ENVISION A YOUNG NICKLAUS STARING AT THIS PORTRAIT AND SEEING HIMSELF IN THE SAME SETTING. EVENTUALLY, HE WAS TO ASCEND TO THE RARIFIED AIR OF JONES BY WINNING FOUR U.S. OPENS, A FEAT ONLY ACCOMPLISHED BY FOUR MEN, WILLIE ANDERSON AT THE TURN OF THE CENTURY, BEN HOGAN IN THE LATE 1940S AND EARLY 1950S, AND JONES HIMSELF IN 1923, 1926, 1929, AND 1930. WAS IT THE LONE PICTURE OF THE TRIUMPHANT JONES THAT SPURRED THIS EFFORT? NO ONE KNOWS, BUT IT COULDN'T HAVE HURT. PHOTO COURTESY OF THE TUFTS ARCHIVES (OF THE GIVEN MEMORIAL LIBRARY)

Bunker, brook, trees, and out of bounds will make double bogey the next step.

A well-struck drive will leave the player a long iron into the green from an uphill lie. This is classic Ross. He believed that only the most skilled golfers could play long irons successfully and thought that this was the most exciting shot in the game. And if excitement is what you seek, the second shot at Scioto's second hole will provide it.

The green is large—with bunkers to the right and left—and raised by some ten feet from the floor of the fairway. There is a small entryway on the right front that will allow the player to run the ball to the green. On this surface, there is nary a straight putt.

Holes like this and the other seventeen at Scioto are a testament to the game of Jack Nicklaus. Most will agree that he mastered this course by his middle teens, before taking his quite considerable game into the record books of golf.

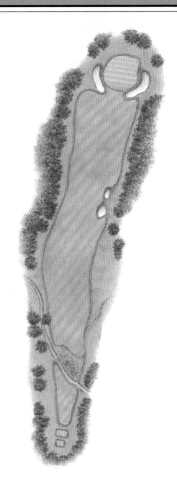

ABOVE: NO. 2, AS ILLUSTRATED BY JOHN BURGOYNE, 2000.
OPPOSITE PAGE: A SHOT OF THE FAIRWAY LOOKING TOWARDS THE TEE.

HERE, THE DECEPTIVE CONTOURS AFFIRM
THAT DONALD ROSS ALWAYS DEFENDED PAR AT
THE GREEN.

A CLASSIC
PITCH HOLE WANNAMOISETT

NUMBER
3

132 YARDS OF AIR TRAVEL TO A BEAUTIFULLY
SHAPED GREEN. GET IT RIGHT THE FIRST TIME.

"As a middle handicap player, I see all the trouble that this course poses. Ross just seemed to know exactly where to place bunkers so that they would catch a bad shot, but not interfere with a good one." Don Paulhus, Wannamoisett club historian

NUMBER

3

WEST NEWTON, MASSACHUSETTS • 1914

132 YARDS • PAR 3

ONE HUNDRED AND thirty-two yards from the tee, the No. 3 is a classic pitch hole. The player could use an eight iron, a nine iron, or a wedge. The green is approximately thirty yards deep and twenty-two paces wide.

Immediately within visibility is a bunker positioned to the left of the green. To the left of the bunker is a cart path and left of the path is a fence that separates the course from Hoyt Avenue. The left bunker is not particularly friendly because the green slopes away from the player. Even a well-hit bunker shot will run to the right side of the green. The smart player will certainly recog-

WANNAMOISETT IS A MIRACULOUS design. Ross built this marvelous course in 1914 and returned to remodel it in 1926. The members of the Wannamoisett Club have consistently striven to preserve Ross's work. After playing the Wannamoisett course about twenty times, I have reached the inescapable conclusion that Wannamoisett is an Indian word that means double bogey. Wannamoisett beats players over the head from the first tee onward. The green speeds at Wannamoisett are typically ten on the stimpmeter, but for tournament play the greens are double cut and rolled, which produces speeds that are difficult to measure. Add to this challenge the herd of dead elephants buried under these surfaces and putting can be a problem for even the best players.

CONTROL THE ROLL OR PREPARE TO PULL OUT
THE WEDGE.

nize that the area left of the green is not desirable.

WANNAMOISETT HAS BEEN THE SITE FOR THE NORTHEAST AMATEUR SINCE 1960. CONSISTENTLY, THIS EVENT DRAWS ABOUT NINETY PERCENT OF THE TOP RANKED AMATEURS IN THE WORLD. WINNERS HAVE INCLUDED BEN CRENSHAW, JOHN COOK, JAY SIGEL AND OTHERS THAT HAVE GONE ON TO FAME IN THE PROFESSIONAL GAME. IN THAT THIRTY-NINE-YEAR SPAN, PAR HAS BEEN BROKEN ONLY TWICE.

Attention then turns to the bunker that fronts the green. This bunker is essentially flat and eminently playable, particularly if the pin is positioned in the front of the green. If the pin is positioned at

the rear of the green, the front bunker is not much of an option in that a bunker shot of this distance is very difficult to gauge. If it is hit too hard the ball will find the area over the green, the dead zone. Here, the grass is long and irregular, and there is a fairly drastic slope upward. Playing out of this area requires familiarity with some of the famous chip shots of golf: the "chili-dip," the "T.C. Chen," and the ever popular "skull."

Next in the player's purview is the area to the right of the green. This is an area that seems to have escaped the attention of the course superintendent. Before the player encounters a very unfriendly stream, approximately twenty feet of long, gnarly, unkempt grass enters the picture. Obviously this area, too, should be avoided.

The thinking player will quickly reach the conclusion that options on the third are nonexistent. The player must hit the green or suffer dire consequences. This

OPPOSITE PAGE: IF YOU END UP HERE, ON THE RIGHT SIDE OF THE GREEN, YOU'RE NOT HAVING A GOOD DAY.

is not a terribly challenging task. After all, the hole is only 132 yards long; it's just a simple pitch.

BEWARE OF
THE DOGLEG BRAE BURN

NUMBER
4

Any player standing on this tee for the first time will start to compile a list of horrors:
out of bounds, tree, bunkers, 437 yards to the green, and bends left to right.

NUMBER
4

WEST NEWTON, MASSACHUSETTS • 1897
437 YARDS • PAR 4

THE CHAMPIONSHIP TEE of No. 4 is built against the western boundary of the course, and the out of bounds travels the length of the hole to the right. This would not normally be an issue but the hole bends ever so softly from left to right. To compound the problem of the slight dogleg, someone placed a tree on the right corner of the fairway about 200 yards from the tee.

The driving sightline is further confused by four medium-sized fairway bunkers placed along the left side at about 230, 240, 250, and 260 yards. The closest bunker is furthest left with its brothers inching to the right successively. The fairway is quite generous, about 35 yards wide.

BRAE BURN HELD two USGA Major Championships in golf's formative years in the United States. These two championships, the 1919 United States Open and the 1928 United States Amateur, were won by the best players of the time. Walter Hagen won in 1919, and Robert Tyre Jones, Jr., was the victor in 1928. The course is landlocked and surrounded by some of the most beautiful old housing I have ever seen. This made it impossible to lengthen the course significantly. Because of its lack of length, Brae Burn has not been employed for any further men's championships, yet it has been the site of the 1958 and 1970 Curtis Cups and the Women's Amateur in 1906, 1975, and 1997.

THE CLUB HOUSE AT BRAE BURN COUNTRY CLUB.

From the tee, the trick is to take a driver at the left bunkers and cut it ever so softly back into the fairway. Believe me, this is much easier to say than to do.

Any drive which misses the fairway by more than a few scant feet will provide the player with only a lay-up option. The fairway bunkers on the left are well constructed and will allow a long iron shot, yet the possibility of gaining purchase on the green from any of the fairway bunkers is not great.

The right side is even more treacherous. The rough on the right side is not conducive to allowing the player to shape the shot, and the angle to the green demands a shot hit left to right.

A good drive will leave the player with some 180 to 210 yards to the green. As on the tee, the player once again gets to review a long list of speed bumps between he or she and the hole. A hundred yards short of the green

OPPOSITE PAGE: STANDING IN THE ROUGH ON THE RIGHT SIDE OF THE FAIRWAY AND LOOKING FOR THE BEST APPROACH TO THE GREEN.

is a bunker that is positioned in the right rough and covers about a third of the fairway. On the left there is a series of bunkers, the first about 45 yards from the green, followed by three others: 25 yards, 15 yards, and greenside. To the right of the green there is a

RIGHT: BRAE BURN HOLE NUMBER 4, AS ILLUSTRATED BY JOHN BURGOYNE, 2000.

greenside bunker, and to the right of it is out of bounds. As with any shot that lands beyond the green, a shot that lands beyond the bunkers will likely travel off the property. If the player intends to fly the ball to the green, the pin must be positioned at the rear.

Approximately 9,000 square feet of terror, the green is a wonder. There are no straight putts. The slope from back to front is predominant and predictable but the other rolls—from right to left and left to right—are not nearly as assured. Judging the speed and break is crucial here.

THE NUMBER ONE STROKE HOLE IN THE WORLD! PINEHURST NO. 2

NUMBER
5

"Course Number 2 is the consummate test in golf. It challenges every component of your game, physically as well as mentally." Lew Ferguson, Golf Operations Manager and Head Professional, Pinehurst Country Club

NUMBER
5

PINEHURST, NORTH CAROLINA • 1901

435 YARDS • PAR 4

WHILE MOST OF Ross's were for member play, Course Number 2 was designed specifically for championship play. It has been the site of the North and South Amateur since 1903. A parallel professional tournament, the North and South Four Ball, was held here for close to 60 years. In addition, Course Number 2 has hosted the U.S. Amateur, the PGA Championship, the Ryder Cup and, most recently, the 1999 United States Open. Suffice to say, every golf champion from Harry Vardon to Tiger Woods has played competitive golf on Pinehurst Number 2. The fifth hole shares with the Road Hole (No. 17) at the Royal and Ancient the distinction of the hardest par four in the world

IN JUNE OF 1999, the fifth hole at Pinehurst managed to keep its distinction as the number one stroke hole in the world. Only 29 rounds of the 448 played produced scores under par. This was in part due to the fact that the eighth and sixteenth holes, which normally play as par fives, were reduced to par fours, bringing par for the course to 70. The fifth hole surrendered a total of 15 birdies in the four days of the Open and played to a higher stroke average than either number eight or sixteen.

IN 2005, THE PLAYERS OF THE U.S. OPEN
CHAMPIONSHIP WILL AGAIN TRY TO CONQUER
ROSS'S MASTERPIECE.

THE PIN WITHIN VIEW, LOOKING BACK AT THE FAIR-
WAY OF ONE OF THE MOST DIFFICULT PAR FOURS IN
THE WORLD.

THE SADDLEBACKED GREEN WITH ITS
ENDLESS SUBTLETIES.

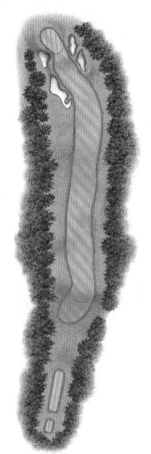

(many will say this is because both are really par fives).

SOME YEARS AGO, THIS AUTHOR WATCHED TWO SENIOR CADDIES ARGUE ARDUOUSLY OVER THE POSSIBILITIES OF A TEN FOOT PUTT. THE ONLY AGREEMENT REACHED WAS THE PUTT WOULD BREAK TWO BALLS. ONE CADDY SAID FROM RIGHT TO LEFT; THE OTHER LEFT TO RIGHT. SPLITTING THE DIFFERENCE, THE PLAYER HIT THE BALL STRAIGHT AND HOLED THE PUTT. MAYBE THERE IS ONE FLAT SURFACE ON THE GREEN.

The tee shot on the fifth hole is blind. A gentle rise in the fairway about 120 yards from it blocks any view of the fairway. Out of bounds lurks far to the right. Trees line the rough far to the left. Only the hazards are evident. The fairway tilts dramatically from right to left, assigning a place in the heavy Bermuda rough to anyone who plays left of center from the tee. Only a precision drive down the right third

of the fairway will provide a viable second shot to the green. It must be added that the drive must not only be well-placed but also well-struck, as a 280-yard poke from the tee leaves 200 yards to the green.

The second shot on this hole is a visual nightmare. Short and right are bunkers, short and left are bunkers, long and right will provide a downhill chip that is not likely to come to rest on the surface. Long and left allows for a visit to

LEFT: HOLE NUMBER 5, AS ILLUSTRATED BY JOHN BURGOYNE, 2000. *ABOVE:* THE CENTER OF ATTENTION—COURSE NUMBER TWO, CIRCA 1940. PHOTO COURTESY OF THE TUFTS ARCHIVES (OF THE GIVEN MEMORIAL LIBRARY)

the great beyond, which will put the ball in the greenside bunker or allow it to roll fifty to sixty feet below the green's surface. These are the thoughts going through the mind of the player who, while holding a three iron, is standing in the fairway with his feet below the ball. If the player is singular minded, tough in spirit, and steeled in experience, he or she will see only the green. Then the fun begins!

The green takes the shape of a gargantuan tortoise standing at a forty-five degree angle with the fairway. From where the second shot is struck, the player can see most of the green's surface, yet what is espied does not appear attainable. In essence, the player sees a great hump arising from the end of the fairway. The fronting of the green is unobstructed but considerably narrowed by the angle. Any shot hit too far to the left will kick left and end up at the base of the hill or into the greenside bunker. Any shot struck too far to the right will pass over the right side of the green and end up in a swale to the right rear. The landing area is five to six paces wide and six to eight paces deep; anything outside this perimeter will not result in a putt. Only a perfectly fashioned shot that is shaped from left to right and on a high trajectory will find the elusive surface.

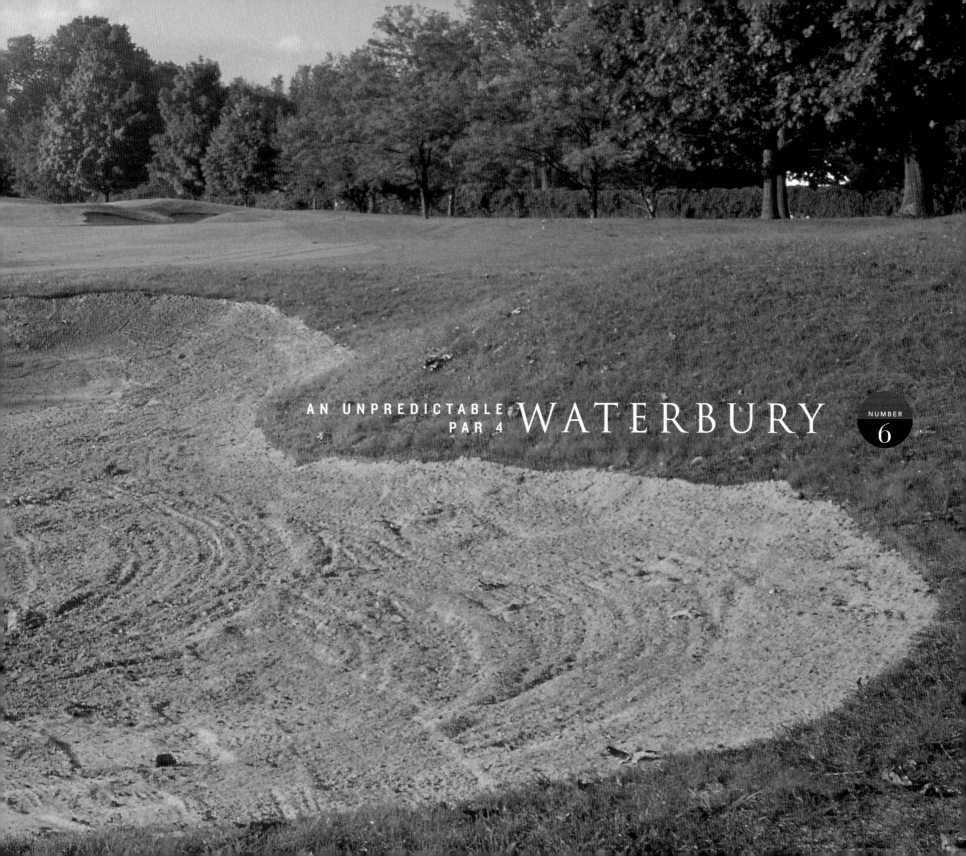

AN UNPREDICTABLE
PAR 4 WATERBURY

NUMBER
6

Too many times has the good player walked off this green after making six and
searching his soul for why the golf gods have once again eaten his lunch.

NUMBER
6

WATERBURY, CONNECTICUT • 1926
300 YARDS • PAR 4

THIS IS A PRIME example of a Ross uphill short four par. From the slightly raised tee, the player is shown a fairly wide and inviting fairway that decreases in width starting 160 yards from the tee. The hole is only 300 yards long, so for a sure second shot from the fairway the player can employ as little as a six or seven iron from the tee.

As the fairway ascends, the hazards begin to appear. All along the right side there are trees that hide the fence to the out of bounds. Anything hit more than fifteen yards right of the fairway is "hastà la vista." The left side of the fairway features four bunkers starting 180 yards from the tee

TO MY KNOWLEDGE, Donald Ross did not endeavor to build any one-shot par fours. He built some pretty rugged three pars (No. 4 at Worcester comes to mind immediately, 246 yards with garrison bunkers in the front). He did, however, engage in the art of the short par four. Many times, Mr. Ross used the short par four to ascend a hill. This strategy was employed at a good number of his courses, including No. 16 at Holston Hills, No. 13 at Pinehurst Course Number 2, No. 2 at Brae Burn (one of the neatest option holes on the planet), No. 5 at Pine Needles, No. 4 at Mid Pines, and No. 14 at Oak Hill East, to name a few. It was often in his playbook to create a short uphill par four as the seventeenth hole to allow for a lofted perch from which to begin the finishing hole. Three good examples of this are Essex Country Club in Massachusetts, Wampanoag in Connecticut, and Bellevue in Syracuse.

FROM THE TEE, THE VIEW OF THE FAIRWAY AND
THE LEFT SIDE BUNKERS.

and guard the left side to 240-plus yards from the tee. Left of the bunkers is death—trees, fescue, and the terrible unknown. There is a bunker on the right side of the fairway that demarks where the hold turns slightly from right to left. This bunker is easily attainable from the tee and must be avoided.

Once the drive has been properly negotiated, the player faces a second shot that requires both accuracy and distance control. The green is open in the front yet raised slightly from the fairway negating the run-up shot as a major option. The ball must be flown on board and, might I say, to the proper quadrant of the green. There are bunkers to the left, right, forward, and aft. They are deep and testy.

This green has no flat spots. It is somewhat saucer-shaped yet not quite so predictable. The hole locations abound, most of which do not offer any type of straight putt from close quarters. Lag putting from twenty feet is at a premium on this green.

Like most Ross greens, the front pin positions are the most difficult to attain. If the player is long on his second, his putt runs the risk of carrying past the front pin right into the fairway. If the player is short, his chip is strikingly uphill and very difficult to judge.

THE GREENS ON THESE SHORT UPHILL HOLES CAN ONLY BE DESCRIBED AS SMALL AND MEAN. THEY ARE USUALLY WELL BUNKERED IN THE FRONT AND SLOPE DRAMATICALLY FROM BACK TO FRONT. THIS MEANS THAT THE PLAYER MUST HIT AN ACCURATELY JUDGED SECOND SHOT OR FACE A BUNKER SHOT OR A SEVERELY DOWNHILL CHIP OR PUTT. THE SECOND SHOT IS COMPOUNDED WITH THE PROBLEM OF AN UPHILL LIE THAT CAUSES TWO FAVORITE MISHITS, THE "PULL" AND THE DREADED "STICK THE CLUB IN THE GROUND" SHOT. THE "STICK THE CLUB IN THE GROUND" SHOT IS ONE OF MY FAVORITES. YOU STEP UP TO THE BALL WITHOUT REALIZING THAT THE STANCE YOU HAVE TAKEN HAS YOUR LEFT SHOULDER POINTED TOWARD THE EARTH. AFTER A SLOW AND DELIBERATE BACKSWING, YOU DELIVER THE CLUB TO THE BACK OF THE BALL. SINCE YOUR SHOULDERS ARE OUT OF ALIGNMENT, RATHER THAN HITTING THE LITTLE WHITE BALL, YOUR CLUB CRASHES MIGHTILY INTO THE BIG GREEN BALL. THE LITTLE WHITE BALL SCAMPERS OFF LIKE A DISTRESSED PUPPY SOME 40 OR 50 YARDS AND YOU ARE FACED WITH THE TASK OF CLEANING FOUR POUNDS OF DIRT OUT OF THE GROOVES OF YOUR NINE IRON AND REPLACING A TWELVE-POUND DIVOT. YOUR NECK REDDENS AND YOU BEGIN TO THINK OF THE MANY MEANS YOU CAN USE TO WIPE THE SMIRK OFF THE FACES OF YOUR OPPONENTS.

OPPOSITE PAGE: THE GREEN DESIGN AT WATERBURY'S HOLE NO. 6 REQUIRES THAT THE ROSS PRINCIPLE OF "GOOD JUDGMENT" BE INCLUDED IN THE PLAYER'S BAG OF TRICKS.

A PRIME OPTION
PAR 5 HOLSTON HILLS

NUMBER
7

ON A SUNNY DAY IN KNOXVILLE, THE TEE
AT NUMBER 7.

Here, Ross makes manifest the true essence of risk/reward.

NUMBER

7

KNOXVILLE, TENNESSEE • 1928

475 YARDS • PAR 5

THE SEVENTH AT Holston Hills is 475 yards long and a prime example of an option par five, as there are two distinct and obvious routes to the hole. As with most properly designed option par fives, the more aggressive route is fraught with danger, but, if successfully navigated, can produce an easy birdie and an honest chance at an eagle. The alternate route is far less onerous and, if played with even mediocre talent, will produce an easy par.

From the tee, approximately 225 yards down the main fairway (the one to the right), are three bunkers that prevent any further forward motion. The fairway is reasonably wide, close to 35 yards. A ball that is pulled or pushed will undoubtedly find the rough, which is not terribly

HOLSTON HILLS is an extraordinary Ross reverie. It is a truly unspoiled walk from the first tee to the eighteenth green, without the interference of any architectural stray. One play of this magnificent course removes all doubt as to why it has been picked for so many important events. Like all great golf courses, it makes the player use all 14 clubs.

THE HAZARDS AT HOLSTON HILLS ARE AS BEAUTI-
FUL AS THEY ARE CHALLENGING.

punitive in that the second shot is a mid-iron lay-up to an area some 100 to 60 yards short of the green.

Taking that route, a 225-yard drive followed by a 175-yard iron shot to the lay-up area presents the player with a wedge shot to the putting surface. This is pretty much plain vanilla, and unless the player badly misplays one of the three shots his reward will be at worst par. If he strikes his third with dexterity, birdie is a possibility.

Plan B, the left side route, is much more interesting. Approximately 175 yards from the tee a patch of short grass begins and is elevated to the extent that the fairway is not within visibility. To the left of the second fairway, from 100 to 225 yards out, is a pond that will gleefully swallow hooked tee shots. The left fairway is not nearly as generous as its brother as it is only about 20 yards wide and is bordered by rough and trees. The daring player who hits the left fairway with authority can take advantage of a slight downhill slope and drive the ball—without peril—some 320 yards. This leaves the option of using a long- to mid-iron to reach an inviting green. Aggressive players must beware of the out-of-bounds that lurks close to the right and long of the green, while keeping in mind that balls hit off downhill lies tend to fly to the right.

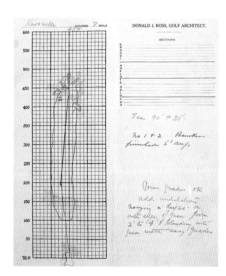

ABOVE: ROSS'S ORIGINAL DESIGN FOR NUMBER 7 AT HOLSTON HILLS, 1927. SINCE THEN, THE HOLE HAS BEEN LENGTHENED BY 17 YARDS. PHOTO COURTESY OF THE TUFTS ARCHIVE (OF THE GIVEN MEMORIAL LIBRARY) OPPOSITE PAGE: A VIEW OF THE NUMBER 7 GREEN AT HOLSTON HILLS, JUST AS THE SUN BEGINS TO WARM ITS SURFACE.

ON THE WAY TO
THE HILL OF FAME OAK HILL EAST

NUMBER
8

Par is a good number at number eight; bogey is survival.

NUMBER
8

ROCHESTER, NEW YORK • 1923
430 YARDS • PAR 4

IT IS UNLIKELY THAT any book written about Donald Ross or the golf courses and holes that he designed could overlook the Oak Hill complex in Rochester, New York.

Oak Hill has not one but two Donald Ross–designed golf courses, the East and West. The West Course is the lesser known of the two, as several major events have been held on the East. West is more original in terms of Ross than the East Course. While the East course's eighth hole is not spectacular unto itself, it is representational of the two Ross layouts at the site.

No. 8 is a 430-yarder, fairly straightaway, with a rise in the fairway that will slow down a

IN MY TRAVELS, I have yet to visit any place that exudes the essence of golf more than the Oak Hill Country Club. The clubhouse, the parking lot, the courses, and especially the trees are all of grand scale. The magnificent oaks that pervade the golf courses are the legacy of Dr. John Williams, a founder of the club and longtime president. Williams, it is told, grew over 10,000 oak trees from acorns in his backyard and transplanted them on the grounds over a thirty-year period. The result is that the holes at Oak Hill, both East and West, are bordered by these giant vertical hazards that steer the player to the playing ground. Oak Hill East has many wonderful golf holes, four of which are exceptionally difficult. The first, a 440-yard par four, and the finish, a 440-yard serpentine par *continued on page 121*

FROM THE TEE, THIS VIEW OF THE FAIRWAY
REVEALS AN IMMEDIATE RISE IN ELEVATION JUST
BEYOND THE NARROW WATER HAZARD.

NUMBER 13 AT OAK HILL, A DASTARDLY PAR 5.
THE OAKS SURROUNDING THIS GREEN CARRY THE
PLAQUES THAT DESIGNATE THE MEMBERS OF THE
"HILL OF FAME."

HERE, A PLAYER ATTEMPTS TO ACCURATELY
NAVIGATE ONE OF THE FASTEST GREENS IN
THE ROSS PORTFOLIO.

poorly hit tee shot. There are bunkers in the diving area both left and right, and trees flanking the outer perimeters on both sides. The rough at Oak Hill is so difficult that it is not impossible to actually lose a golf ball just a few steps out of the fairway.

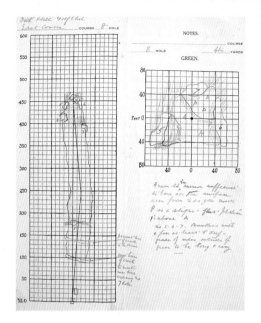

A well-struck, well-positioned drive will leave a long- to mid-iron to a slightly elevated green. Negotiating the opening on the left front of the green is the easiest way home. The right front and side are bunkered, as is the left side. The greens are notoriously hard and fast at both Oak Hill courses, so any second shot hit too hard will find its way to the back of the green. If this is the case, the player will need to employ his

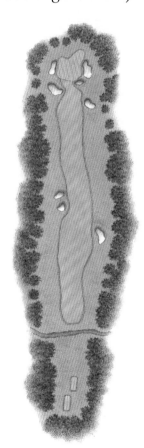

very best feel to get down in two. If the player overclubs significantly, the ball will roll over and down. From there the player should just mail in his resignation.

continued from page 114 four with an uphill finish, qualify as the most difficult opener/closer combination in the game. The two par five holes, Number 4 at 570 yards, and 13 at 594 yards, are two of the elite five pars where five is actually a good number. These two monsters have held their respective heads high under the assault of players in three U.S. Opens, the U.S. Amateur, the Ryder Cup, and the PGA Championship. More than once, bogey won the 13th at Oak Hill East in the 1995 Ryder Cup. The stately oaks that surround the thirteenth green at Oak Hill East comprise the Hill of Fame. The Hill is a collection of plaques attached to a large oak that commemorate and celebrate the lives and achievements of many of the greats of the game. The installation of a new member of the Hill of Fame is done in a solemn and serious fashion preceded by a procession from the clubhouse. I was one of the lucky participants in this walk in 1995 when Byron Nelson was inducted in celebration of the fiftieth anniversary of his 18 victories (11 straight) in 1945. The previous year, my hair stood on end when I walked with the Hill of Fame Committee and invited guests to install the plaque of Donald J. Ross.

AN ALL-OR-
NOTHING HOLE POINT JUDITH

NUMBER
9

FROM HERE, JUST BEYOND THE TEE, THE TARGET APPEARS WELL WITHIN REACH.

Perparing for the Turn.

NUMBER
9

NARAGANSETT, RHODE ISLAND • 1927

120 YARDS • PAR 3

GOLF IS A GAME of what is to come. The most important shot in the game, according to Ben Hogan, is the next one. Never is this truer than near the turn. A player can have a very lackadaisical front side and make the turn and set the world on fire. This has happened over and over again, especially in major championship play.

Nine is a frame-of-mind hole. A positive attitude is necessary to rally from any deficit. A determination to play aggressively and without fear must be attained to carry the player to greater accomplishments and victory on the latter half of the golf course. If the player lacks

POINT JUDITH is located on one of the premier properties in all of golf: the southeastern point of Rhode Island. A rudimentary nine-hole course was built there around the turn of the century to cater to the summer colony visitors at Narragansett and other nearby beach communities. Ross was hired in 1927 to remodel the original course and add nine additional holes. The club is splendid in its simplicity. It is small, elegant, and efficient. Unlike most country clubs, Point Judith refuses to compete with the local restaurants, opening only for lunch. The clubhouse's veranda, a popular socializing spot, offers beautiful views of the ocean and the golf course.

THE HIGH WINDS ON THIS PENINSULA MAKE FOR
SHORT STICKS FOR PINS.

THE ONE ADVANTAGE TO AN ALL-OR-NOTHING
HOLE IS THAT ANY BALL ON THE GREEN IS A
POTENTIAL ONE-PUTT.

determination on the ninth tee, he or she should quit at the turn. If the fire is not burning by then, no incendiary device will be able to produce a flame later on.

WHEN WE WATCH THE MASTERS ON THURSDAY, FRIDAY, AND SATURDAY, THE ANNOUNCERS OFTEN SAY THAT THE REAL TOURNAMENT BEGINS ON THE BACK SIDE ON SUNDAY. NEVER HAS THIS BEEN THIS MORE EFFECTIVELY PROVEN THAN WHEN, IN 1986, FORTY-SIX-YEAR-OLD JACK NICKLAUS PLAYED THE BACK AT AUGUSTA NATIONAL IN AN UNBELIEVABLE THIRTY STROKES TO OVERTAKE THE FIELD AND WIN HIS SIXTH GREEN JACKET. JACK'S CHARGE IS THAT OF THE LEGEND WHICH IS JACK. BUT THE CHARGE HE MADE THAT DAY STARTED ON THE NINTH, WHERE HE MADE BIRDIE TO SET THE STAGE ON THE PLAYING FIELD AND BEHIND HIS BABY BLUES.

The ninth at Point Judith is a wonderful stage for the demonstration of courage and determination. It is an all-or-nothing hole. At 127 yards in length, it is not out of the reach of any golfer. The green is attainable even to those sorely lacking the talent necessary for championship play. The player must ascend the tee, choose a

LEFT, HOLE NUMBER 9 AT POINT JUDITH, AS ILLUSTRATED BY JOHN BURGOYNE, 2000.

weapon, peer at the target, zero in on the pin, and convince one's self that the shot is within reach. The green is small. The bunker in front is menacing, and the areas to the left and right should be avoided. The only option is to relax, concentrate, and pull the trigger. We'll see you on the back side.

OPPOSITE PAGE: THE ONLY POSSIBLE CHANCE FOR PAR, OTHER THAN THE GREEN, IS THIS FRONT BUNKER.

A STRAIGHTAWAY 442-YARD PAR FOUR **THE SAGAMORE**

justice *n.* **1** In 1985, every detail of The Sagamore golf course
was fully restored according to Donald Ross's original blueprints.

LAKE GEORGE, NEW YORK • 1928
442 YARDS • PAR 4

THE TENTH AT THE SAGAMORE is a wonderful 442-yard par four that emanates from a tee that is pushed back into the trees. It is essentially a straightaway hole with trees on both the left and right. At about 240 yards from the tee, there is a fairly dramatic downhill descent of approximately 100 feet to where the ground flattens and then rises ever so slightly to the green. The proper tee shot is a fairway metal to the top of the rise. A fairway bunker on the left should be

DESIGNED AND BUILT IN 1928, The Sagamore is a marvelous, difficult venue that is a feat of early-day engineering. The property is located about a mile up a hill that overlooks Lake George. The resort's hotel is a magnificent affair designed and built in the early part of the twentieth century. In the early part of the 1980s, the hotel and resort fell into disrepair. The elderly owner of the resort was approached by the local fire marshal and told that the hotel would have to make significant upgrades to pass the muster of the fire code. Rumor has it that the owner was less than enthusiastic about this prospect and invited the fire marshal to avail himself of a visit to Lake George. In 1983 the grand hotel, The Sagamore, closed, and with it the facilities that surrounded it. Included in this inventory was its golf course. Abandoned and left to the elements, The Sagamore was allowed to return to nature. And it did so with a vengeance. In 1987 a group of businessmen got together and decided to revive the hotel. They bought the property and began a fifty-million-dollar restoration campaign. Few restorations have been so successful. When they got around to the golf course, they found that a good deal of its definition had been lost. Bunkers were growing grass and weeds, fairways had become grazing areas, and greens sported trees with trunks of two inches in diameter. A golf course architect was called in to consult on the property. He promptly suggested changes and a strategy for building a course. Still unsure of how to proceed, the management team waited. While on a trip to the *continued on page 137*

VIEW OF THE FAIRWAY AT NO. 10 AS IT RISES
TOWARD THE GREEN.

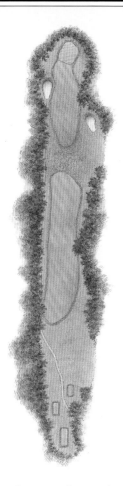

avoided. This will leave a seven- or eight-iron to the putting surface. If the player is too aggressive off the tee, there is no reward. The longer drive will catch a severe downhill lie that leaves the player's feet somewhat below the ball.

THE MOST REMARKABLE FEATURE OF THIS HOLE IS THAT IT WAS DESIGNED AND BUILT IN THE 1920S AND WAS PLAYABLE THEN. THE GREEN IS ON NEARLY THE LOWEST POINT OF THE PROPERTY. ROSS MANAGED TO POSITION THE GREEN SITE ON SUCH A LOW POINT AND MAKE IT PLAYABLE THROUGH A VERY CLEVER DRAINAGE SCHEME. THE GREEN IS ONLY SLIGHTLY ELEVATED FROM THE FAIRWAY FLOOR, YET IT IS SLOPED IN SUCH A FASHION THAT THE WATER ROLLS OFF THE FRONT OF IT AND THROUGH THE BUNKER ON THE LEFT. THE AREA SHORT OF THE GREEN IS WET MOST OF THE TIME, BUT THE GREEN IS PLAYABLE EVEN AFTER THE HEAVIEST OF RAINFALL. ROSS CERTAINLY MADE THE BEST USE OF THE PROPERTY AT THE SAGAMORE.

The green is a little offset to the right, making it even more difficult to reach the target from a hook stance. A bunker guards the left side of the green. Left of the bunker brings the forest into play. The right side of the green is mounded; right of the mound is impossible. The green is large—about 5,500 square feet—with a

LEFT: THE SAGAMORE'S NO. 10, AS ILLUSTRATED BY JOHN BURGOYNE, 2000 OPPOSITE PAGE: THE BRILLIANTLY RESTORED GREEN AT NO. 10

decided slope from back to front and left to right. The right side rises fairly dramatically just ten or so feet

from the edge. There are no easy two-putts on this green from beyond twenty feet.

continued from page 134 island of Bermuda, one member made the acquaintance of Tom Smack, then director of golf at Bermuda's Castle Harbor Resort. Smack was a respected member of the PGA and was also considered one of the best golf directors in the business. The partner implored him to visit The Sagamore and consult on their restoration project. After due deliberation, he agreed to take a look. Once there, it took him about ten minutes to declare, "This is a Donald Ross course." Soon thereafter, the process of restoration began. A local construction firm with experience in shaping and grading was employed. The bones of the original course were there, making it easy for the construction firm to follow the existing forms and rebuild the course as it once was. Smack was offered the job of director of golf at The Sagamore but decided to return to the sunny climes of Bermuda. The persistent management of The Sagamore knew that they had stumbled across a great asset in Smack and returned to Bermuda to try to convince him to return to New York. Tom can now be found at The Sagamore's pro shop on a regular basis. The reconstruction done during his watch is to be greatly admired.

HONEST AND
FORTHRIGHT ESSEX

NUMBER
11

"Ross was hired as club pro here in 1909. Before teeing off at Number 11, give some serious thought to your club selection." Tom Yee, Golf Assistant, Essex County Club

MANCHESTER, MASSACHUSETTS • 1893
176 YARDS • PAR 3

LIKE MOST OF Ross's holes, the eleventh is honest and forthright and right in front of the player. There are no hidden hazards, no deceptive hollows, just a majestic little 176-yard par three built into a hill.

From the tee this hole looks rather pretty and fairly docile. The green is elevated some 20 to 25 feet from the tee. Three bunkers are in view; one short and left of the green and two enormous ones to the right, separated by a path. The two large bunkers cover some 5,000 square feet and are strategically placed to confound the player.

The green has a slope from back to front and from right to left. Anything hit from the tee to

I PLAYED ESSEX ONLY TWICE, once in 1990 and again in 1993. I can remember the feeling of anticipation the second time out as we went from tee to green, hole to hole. My memory of the holes was nearly exact. My memory of the golf values was almost without error. In both 1990 and 1993 I managed to use each of the fourteen clubs in my bag before stepping to the tenth tee.

THE GREAT BEAUTY THAT IS THE ESSEX COUNTY
CLUB IS THE FEELING THAT THE GOLF COURSE
WAS MOWN FROM THE NATURAL LAND.

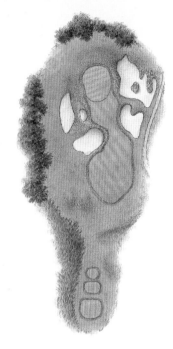

the left quadrant will most assuredly run off the left side of the putting surface, down a 30-foot embankment to a graveyard of fescue and trees. Any ball hit to this area will return—at very best—a four to the player. A shot that is hit poorly and left from the tee will find the left front bunker and provide similar results.

This leaves the player with a certain trepidation of the left side, which will often cause him to block his tee shot into either the Sahara or the Gobi, the bunkers on the right. Of the two, the second bunker, which is even with the center of the green, is the lesser evil. The green height bunker is no "day at the beach" in that there is a six- to seven-foot slope from the back of the green to the front. The right side short bunker provides for a 35- to 40-yard bunker shot to a green that rolls away from the player.

This hole can be played successfully in one of two manners. A shot placed short of the green will run up to the bottom of the putting surface and give the player an even chance for par. The more aggressive line is to play to the middle of the green and pray for a short uphill birdie putt. Any ball that comes to rest above the hole on the "dance floor" almost ensures a three putt.

THE GRANDDADDY OF
ROSS PAR FIVES PLAINFIELD

NUMBER
12

It is often said about a par three or a difficult par four that the player would take par and go to the next tee. This par five appears to have made it into that category.

PLAINFIELD, NEW JERSEY • 1916

585 YARDS • PAR 5

NUMBER TWELVE, a 585-yarder, is the granddaddy of the Ross par fives. From the tee—positioned hard against the right side of the hole—all that can be seen is rough and trees to the right and left, a fairly generous fairway, and a severe drop in elevation approximately 250 yards out. The trick here is to hit the ball straight down the left side of the fairway and catch the roll off the hill. This will move the ball some 320 yards from the tee. If the tee shot strays to the right, the distance will be gained but the second shot will be blocked by a massive mound that rises inelegantly out of the fairway. If the player leaves his drive at the top of the hill, the difficulty of the second shot increases significantly. Running down the right side of the fairway through the

PLAINFIELD COUNTRY CLUB can only be described as a monster. The overall length of the course is 6,850 yards, which is not overbearing. When one removes the two par three holes that are under 150 yards and the five par fours that are under 400 yards (three of which are 299, 345, and 366), this leaves over 4,800 yards for the remaining 11 holes.

THIS VIEW FROM THE NO. 12 TEE REVEALS A FAIR-
WAY WITH SEVERE TILT AND A SIGNIFICANT DROP
IN ELEVATION.

VISIBLE FROM THIS VIEWPOINT IS THE STREAM
THAT CROSSES THE FAIRWAY AND RUNS ALONG
THE SIDE OF THE GREEN.

rough is a stream that crosses into the fairway. At about 130 yards from the green, the stream bends 45 degrees from right to left for about 30 yards. After crossing the fairway, the stream makes a right-hand turn and continues past the left side of the green.

The second shot on this hole is the real key. If the player has managed to eclipse the hill with his drive, he has three options: he can lay up short of the stream in the middle of the fairway, play to the right fairway over the stream, or go straight at the hole by carrying over the stream. The option chosen

RIGHT: ROSS'S ORIGINAL DRAWING AND NOTES FOR PLAIN-FIELD'S HOLE NO. 12, 1915. PHOTO COURTESY OF TUFTS ARCHIVES (OF THE GIVEN MEMORIAL LIBRARY)

most often is dictated by the position of the pin. If the pin is to the left of the green, the play over the stream to the right provides the best angle. If the pin is positioned at the front of the green, the straightaway lay-up is the most logical approach. If the pin is in the rear, the time to go for it is nigh.

The green is a little shop of horrors and only the strongest of players can reach it in two. The smartest players will position the second shot for maximum oppor-tunity. Like most Ross greens, straight putts are nonexistent and the slope from

LEFT: NUMBER 12 AT PLAINFIELD COUNTRY CLUB, AS ILLUS-TRATED BY JOHN BURGOYNE, 2000. OPPOSITE PAGE: THE NUM-BER 12 GREEN—NARY A STRAIGHT PUTT ON ITS SURFACE.

back to front, combined with expert greenkeeping tech-niques, makes any downhill attempt a nightmare.

340 YARDS IS ALL THE DISTANCE NECESSARY FOR A GREAT PAR FOUR SALEM

NUMBER
13

"I look out from my office window and consistently see the same guys playing here; some almost every day. Their love for this course is a testimonial to the greatness of Donald Ross's work here at Salem." Paul Guidi, General Manager, Salem Country Club

NUMBER
13

PEABODY, MASSACHUSETTS • 1925

340 YARDS • PAR 4

FROM THE VERY back of the tees, hard against the northern boundary of the course, this hole measures 340 yards. The ideal shot from the tee is about 200 yards into the middle of the fairway. This leaves the player with approximately 140 yards uphill to the green. Unlike most of Ross's fairway designs, this one is hidden from the tee; all the player can see is the area to the left of it.

The fairway is bowl-shaped and not too small to be a reasonable target, especially when you consider the player is driving with anything from a one to a four iron. To the far right is out-of-bounds. Approximately 190 yards in is a fairly severe fairway bunker that can force even the best players to play safe rather than to the green. To the right of it is a hillside that is severely sloped and covered with long, matted, rough grass. To the left is a hillside to complement the one

A CLEAR VIEW OF WHAT TO AVOID ON NO. 13: A
GREENSIDE HILL FEATURING DEEP, MATTED GRASS.

on the right. Unless the golfer is inordinately lucky and finds an easily playable lie, moving the ball from the left or right rough to the green is nearly impossible.

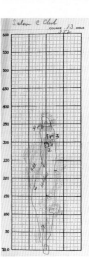

Uphill at about a 60-foot gradual climb, the second shot is an endeavor that takes a great deal of consideration. The green is severely crowned, so any bunker shot will have to be precise to get close to the hole. Short and left of the green is a bunker. The right of the green provides a steep drop-off to fescue and certain consternation. Up and down from this area is unheard of. Over the green is just plain dead. Any ball

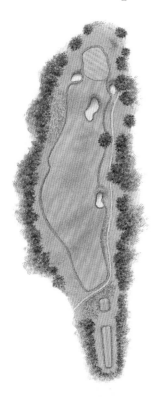

that gets away over the green will be lost to the forest behind it. Thus, the player who hits the ball over the green will do just as well to pick it up, tee it up on 14, and keep going.

A well-struck short iron will find the putting surface but will not ensure par for the player, as the green is simply a terror. A ridge runs through the middle of the putting surface from front to back. The area left of the ridge is the high ground and slopes gradually to the left. The front right of the green is the most accessible from the fairway. The pin positions on the front right are probably the easiest on the hole, but any ball hit past the pin will leave the player with a difficult downhill putt. The front right is no utopia for the *OPPOSITE PAGE:* THE BUNKERS THAT PROTECT THE GREEN AT SALEM COUNTRY CLUB'S HOLE NO. 13 player, especially if the pin is on the left side, particularly the left rear. It is eminently possible for the player to three putt from the area short of the ridge.

As difficult as the left rear of the thirteenth green may be, the right rear of the green is worse. A second ridge runs from the bisecting ridge to the edge of the green causing the right rear to slope fairly dramatically to the right. Nothing will stop the ball from rolling right off the green and down the slope. Putts from all different angles will move on their own momentum, most often without the desired effect. To hole a putt to the left rear pin position, the ball must be hit on the proper line with authority; otherwise the result will be disastrous. The thirteenth at Salem proves that 340 yards is all the distance necessary for a great par four.

THE FINISH
BEGINS THE ORCHARDS

NUMBER
14

Exercise caution at The Orchards. Three-foot tap-ins do not exist here.

NUMBER
14

SOUTH HADLEY, MASSACHUSETTS • 1922

329 YARDS • PAR 4

THE FOURTEENTH HOLE at any course is important due to its position on the course—the beginning of the finish. There is still time on the fourteenth to rally and win a match-play match if only one or two down. In Stroke Play, the fourteenth can be crucial as a hole that will signal a comeback or preserve a round that has been played well.

The fourteenth at The Orchards can be viewed from either point of view. It can be played aggressively for birdie or conservatively for par. In either case, it should be played cautiously to avoid disaster.

ON THE GROUNDS OF Mount Holyoke College resides one of the most original Ross courses in existence. The Orchards began as a nine-hole course built by a local indusrialist in 1922 to give his daughter—a promising young golf enthusiast—a place to hone her skills. In 1931, Ross returned to the site and added an additional nine holes. The course has been operated as a semiprivate golf facility since its inception. In more recent years, the course has been operated by Mount Holyoke College, usually at a financial loss. Because of this lack of capital and the general reverence *continued on page 167*

FROM THE FAIRWAY, THE RIGHT-SIDE VIEW OF
THE GREEN AT THE ORCHARDS

VIEW OF THE GREEN, WITH THE ASCENDING FAIRWAY IN THE BACKGROUND.

The drive at The Orchards' fourteenth is crucial. There are woods that encroach upon the rough on either side of the fairway. Finding these trees will ensure a bogey at minimum. The rough is not particularly friendly either. And because the green is not terribly large, a well-struck ball from the rough will not easily stop on its hard surface. The aggressive line on this hole is down the right center of the fairway. From there the green opens up to the player. The conservative left side of the fairway, which is bunkered some 220 yards from the tee, only provides the front of the green as a target.

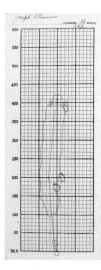

LEFT: THE ORIGINAL ROSS DRAWING OF THE ORCHARDS' FOURTEENTH, CIRCA 1921. PHOTO COURTESY OF TUFTS ARCHIVES (OF THE GIVEN MEMORIAL LIBRARY) OPPOSITE PAGE: A BEAUTIFULLY MANICURED APPROACH AREA TO A GREEN THAT CAN BE LIGHTNING QUICK.

Nearing the green there are a number of hazards to be avoided. Short and right is a bunker that spells real trouble for the weak fade from the fairway. The left side of the green sports a bunker from which the green is straight downhill. Right of the green is a natural area uncut since the days of the local Indians. The area beyond the green is so unsavory that it cannot be fully described in mere words.

Small, tilted, and angry in appearance, the green will surprise you.

continued from page 162 particular layout enjoys, it has largely escaped the ravages of updating and renovation. Two of the greens here have been changed; otherwise, the course remains mostly intact. Recently Mount Holyoke College entered into an agreement with the Arnold Palmer Management Company to run The Orchards. Rumor has it that they will market it as a high-end, daily-fee golf course. They certainly have the right layout for that plan. We at the Donald Ross Society hope that they will honor the designer by simply cutting the grass and leaving the design intact.

THE LONG
ROAD HOME INVERNESS

NUMBER
15

VIEW FROM THE TEE AT INVERNESS

"You'd better have some stuff on the ball at Inverness or it's going to wind up at a place
you don't want to be." Hubert Green, former PGA champion

NUMBER
15

TOLEDO, OHIO • 1920
465 YARDS • PAR 4

FROM THE TEE, the player could well believe that fifteen is really a par five. The hole is 465 yards long and plays somewhat downhill, but requires that the player possess the ability to drive the ball exceptionally well. Within view—about 230 yards to the left—is a horseshoe-shaped bunker that is in play and should be avoided. This is a disastrous place to have to play a second shot, as the chances are strong that it will find the stream that crosses the fairway 100 yards from the hole. About 280 yards to the right is another flatter, rounder bunker, yet at 185 yards from the green it is no less formidable.

OHIO HAS 32 ROSS-designed golf courses, all of which were designed and built before 1932. This is a pretty remarkable number considering that the means of transportation during this period was not conducive to traveling repeatedly from New England to North Carolina to the heartland. From Acacia Country Club in Lyndhurst to Zaneville Country Club in Zaneville, Ross club members in the Buckeye State are proud of their heritage. None are more proud than those who are members of Inverness. Since 1920, The Open has returned to Inverness three times, in 1931, 1957, and 1979. Add to that list the U.S. Amateur of 1973 and the PGA Championships of 1986 and 1993, and the resume of Inverness is complete.

THE HORSESHOE-SHAPED BUNKER AT NO.
15—KNOWN FOR PULLING IN GOLF BALLS LIKE
A VACUUM

THE CLUB HOUSE AT INVERNESS

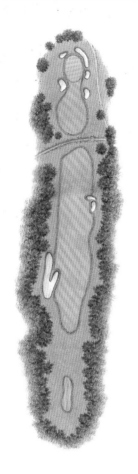

The perfect tee shot is down the right side of the fairway into a little depression that hurries the ball farther toward the target. This little slot is about 240 yards from the tee and will propel the orb to about 175 yards from the green. From here the player has a mid-iron shot to a very, very small target. The green is 21 yards

deep and 19 yards wide, allowing a meager 3,500 square feet of putting surface at which to aim. To further complicate matters, the green is nearly an island in a sea of sand. The right front, the right rear, and the left side of the green have bunkers in place allowing for only a small run-up area on the left side. The green is mild in slope.

Inverness, like many of Ross's championship courses, has been altered to some degree to accommodate championship play. The alterations have invariably made the venue more difficult and more testing. Still,

without the wonderful basic bones laid out by Ross, this would not be possible.

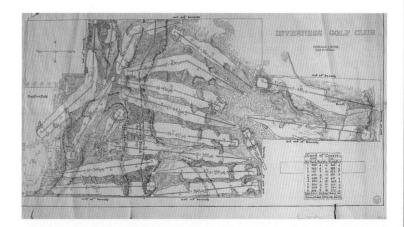

KNOW YOUR
LAY-UP SHOT HARTFORD

NUMBER
16

You're almost to the clubhouse. This is your last very good opportunity to make a
birdie or even an eagle. Know your limitations.

WEST HARTFORD, CONNECTICUT • 1896

475 YARDS • PAR 5

THE SIXTEENTH HOLE runs south to north, about 475 yards tee to green. At the 300-yard mark, the land begins a gradual slope upward which increases dramatically as it reaches the green. To complicate matters, as the slope climbs, the fairway tilts more and more severely from left to right. The green is perched atop the hill and only the front of the putting surface is visible from the fairway. The strategic approach to this hole is crucial to the player.

Standing on the tee, the player sees a fairly generous fairway which is girded on both sides by heavy rough and trees. The trees are closer on the right side and the driving area slopes ever

HARTFORD GOLF CLUB over the years has seen a good deal of change. Today, this very good 27-hole facility is the result of the work of a number of golf architects. After Ross came Devereaux Emmett, David and William Gordon, Orrin Smith, William Mitchell, Robert Trent Jones, Geoffrey Cornish, and William G. Robinson. All plied their trade on the original and later the modified park. In 1995, Stephen Kay was hired by the club to prepare it for the U.S. Mid Amateur. Although many times this hodgepodge approach to architecture fails miserably, thanks to the work of Kay, the Hartford Golf Club is an exception.

THE UPHILL, TILTED, AND WELL-BUNKERED
FAIRWAY OF HARTFORD'S HOLE NO. 16.

so slightly from left to right. A drive hit into the rough on either side will produce a situation whereby the player will have to lay-up with his second shot. Only a well-struck tee shot in excess of 270 yards, that finds itself in the fairway, will provide the long hitter with the GO sign.

The lay-up shot is the real test on this hole. The fairway narrows as one gets closer to the green, ending with a run-up area of approximately twelve yards at the left front of the green. There are two very nasty fairway bunkers adjacent to the left of the fairway, 100 and 70 yards from the green. In addition to these two chasms is an even larger, deeper bunker 90 yards short on the right. This is a very popular resting ground for the weakly struck second shot. The second must thread the needle to produce a favorable situation for the approach.

The green is long and narrow as it faces the fairway. It is cut into the hill which produces a decided roll from left to right. To compound matters, the front of the green slopes towards the back, and the back towards the front. This means that even a two-foot putt from above the hole is no sure bet. Oftentimes a two foot tap-in will produce a six-foot come-back putt.

The short hitter should aim toward the middle of the fairway off the tee, strike a long- to mid-iron up the left center of the fairway from there, and pitch cautiously to the left side of the green. Three well-placed shots will most often present a decent birdie attempt.

The long hitter must take his drive up the left side of the fairway so that his second is from the left or middle of the fairway. He will need to conjure up all of his

confidence to play his second. He must play a fairway metal or long

iron up the left side of the slope and allow the ball to land in the less-than-generous run-up area.

If he attains the green, eagle is a possibility.

THE LONG-IRON GAME WORCESTER

GAME

NUMBER
17

PARTICULARLY FOR THE PLAYER NEW TO THE
COURSE AT WORCESTER, ROSS'S DESIGN FOR
HOLE NO. 17 CAN BE VERY INTIMIDATING.

Warning Ahead: Trees. Heavy rough. Deception.

NUMBER
17

WORCESTER, MASSACHUSETTS • 1913

452 YARDS • PAR 4

FROM AN ELEVATED TEE, the player sees a generous fairway that drops off dramatically on both the left and right. Neither direction is preferable as a bailout because both sides present a frightful side-hill lie covered with trees and heavy rough. Any ball hit more than five yards out of the fairway will have no chance of reaching the green.

At about 260 yards, the fairway drops dramatically back to the low point of the course. In the next 180 yards, the fall off is approximately 230 feet. If the player has driven well, the next shot will have to be a precision long iron. The aim and execution of the second shot will tell

WORCESTER COUNTRY CLUB is one of the forgotten greats. The club was the site for the first Ryder Cup in 1927. In the 1960s it appeared perennially in the top 100 of the course rating lists. With the proliferation of newer, more spectacular courses, Worcester slipped annually until it finally disappeared. Worcester is unimpressed and for that matter unchanged. The history of the course is old, too old for many of the latter-day golf course raters and reporters.

THE DOWNHILL FAIRWAY APPROACH TO THE GREEN. WHEN ROSS DESIGNED THIS HOLE, HE MUST HAVE BEEN THINKING OF HIS FONDNESS FOR THE LONGER IRONS.

whether the player will face a putt, a chip, or a difficult bunker shot. The tendency on downhill lies is to push the ball to the right. Here, a bunker is positioned to catch the

errant shot to the right. Another bunker, short and to the left, will accept anything that is pulled. The best way to the green is to play a shot that lands short and runs to it. Of course, if the shot is too long, there is little that can be done to attain par. If the shot comes up short, only the most delicate chip will bail out the player. The green is deceptively sloped, following the contours of the two major hills. Even if the player has attained green purchase in two, par can be elusive.

OPPOSITE PAGE: STANDING BEHIND THE SLOPED GREEN, LOOK-ING UPHILL AT THE FAIRWAY

THE FEARSOME
FINALE WAMPANOAG

NUMBER
18

"The greatest of champions have all been ex-chokers." Peter Dobreiner

NUMBER
18

WEST HARTFORD, CONNECTICUT • 1919

430 YARDS • PAR 4

FINISHING HOLES ARE oftentimes the most important hole on the golf course. Professional and amateur stroke play tournaments always end on the eighteenth. Sometimes the winner is already determined because of a commanding lead. Most often, however, this is not the case. In a stroke play event at the Wampanoag Country Club, a lead of less than three strokes does not ensure victory standing on the tee. In match play events, the eighteenth can be the ultimate test. Any match tied or one up in either player's favor must continue on the eighteenth.

Let us stand on the eighteenth tee and take a mental inventory. Before you lies a vast and

IF THE PIN IS POSITIONED at the rear of the green, the wind is against the player at about fifteen miles per hour. From fifty feet below the pin, the line must be garnered and the stroke must be pure. The player must propel the ball up the slope to the hole and try to make it stop within a few feet. If the ball is hit more than a couple of feet beyond the pin, the player has just entered the "vomit zone." The vomit zone is that hideous position where the player realizes that if he misses the putt, there is a very good possibility that his next one could be as long as ten feet. Chances of conversion of this little monster are nil. The vomit zone was named in honor of those putts that make even the greatest players throw up on themselves as they contemplate the task ahead. In this golfers' *continued on page 199*

PEEKING THROUGH THE TREES AT THE
EIGHTEENTH TEE

OPPOSITE PAGE: FROM BEHIND THE TREES JUST OFF THE LEFT SIDE OF THE FAIRWAY, THE EIGHTEENTH GREEN APPEARS TO BE WITHIN REACH.

inviting fairway. You are elevated approximately 30 feet from the playing ground. To the right of the fairway is gnarly rough that extends some twelve yards to a lateral water hazard. To the left of the fairway is another generous serving of heavy rough. Approximately ten yards off the fairway are a number of pines that spell real trouble. In the distance is a prominent water hazard where the continuation of the fairway would naturally occur. Your mind captures this scene and also tells you that your drive must be a minimum of 250 yards to afford a sensible second shot. This is the moment of truth.

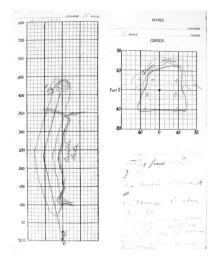

ABOVE: ROSS'S ORIGINAL DRAWING FOR THE EIGHTEENTH HOLE AT WAMPANOAG COUNTRY CLUB, CIRCA 1918. PHOTO COURTESY OF THE TUFTS ARCHIVES (OF THE GIVEN MEMORIAL LIBRARY)

The green is 65 feet above the fairway and close to 40 paces deep. The difference between the front and rear of the green is two clubs. Because it is situated on the high point of the property, a wind into the golfer or from the left will knock the ball down. The steep slope that fronts the green is cut close so that any ball that fails to climb the green level will roll some 40 yards down the slope. The green is also severely sloped from back to front. Thus, the player does not want to go past the hole. Gauging these factors properly is crucial.

continued from page 196 twilight zone the mind goes blank and, if not blank, it can only focus on what can go wrong. Hands that have held the putter for many decades lose all feeling, knees become jelly, breathing becomes irregular, and resolve turns to confusion. Ben Hogan suffered from it, as did Tom Watson and Bernhard Langer, along with thousands of lesser–known players, both professional and amateur. The "vomit zone" is complicated further by the "yips," the unsavory inability to draw the putter straight back and push it straight through. The yips provoke the left wrist to break and the putter head to go off line. I have seen the yips literally paralyze well-seasoned players.

Putting the eighteenth green at Wampanoag requires a very deft touch, coupled with a sensible approach. The player must calculate the maximum break and then endeavor to hit the putt with the exact speed. This will produce a result of either a made putt or a tap-in second putt.

To sum up the eighteenth at Wampanoag (or any other course for that matter), one must remember that golf is 90 percent mental. The other half is physical. (My apologies to Yogi Berra.)

FROM TUFTS TO BELLS: A FAMILY AFFAIR
PINE NEEDLES & MID PINES

DONALD ROSS SPENT the last 48 years of his life as a resident of Pinehurst, NC. He summered in the north, first in Massachusetts, later in Little Compton, RI. As the Pinehurst Resort grew, it became obvious that the four courses that Ross had created there were inadequate for both the visitors and the permanent residents.

In 1921, business at the Pinehurst Resort was actually too good. Many of the long-time visitors sought to return to earlier times when the activities at the hotel were less lively. In response to this need, Leonard Tufts (son of Pinehurst founder James Walker Tufts), Donald Ross, and other prominent Pinehurst–based denizens founded the Mid Pines Club.

The new club was to be built on land that Tufts had acquired about four miles east of the

HOLE NO. 18 AND THE MID PINES HOTEL

Pinehurst Resort. A hotel was erected to house the members of the new club. By 1926 the Mid Pines project proved to be such a success that Richard Tufts, a handful of local businessmen, and a few repeat visitors decided to establish another new club. Located directly across the street from the Mid Pines Club, Pine Needles' construction began in 1927. The course and the first cabin hotel were finished and opened in 1928.

The timing for this opening was less than salubrious. Black Tuesday came in 1929 and the Pine Needles Resort was in dire financial straits. For that matter, the Mid Pines Resort also became a financial drain on the Pinehurst Resort. During the 1930s, both Mid Pines and Pine Needles were sold to alleviate the pressure on the Pinehurst Resort. In the late 1940s, the Pine Needles Hotel was sold to the Catholic Church, and in 1953 the golf course was sold to a young couple from Ohio, Warren and Peggy Kirk Bell. Mid Pines was sold to the Cosgrove family in 1955 and later again to a hotel chain. In the 1990s, Mid Pines was bought by an investment group headed by Peggy Kirk Bell. By 1995, Mid Pines and Pine Needles were once again united as a family operation, no longer the Tufts but, rather, the Bells.

Some might assume that two courses—across the street from each other—built six years

OPPOSITE PAGE: HOLE NO. 3, A SIGNATURE HOLE AT PINE NEEDLES

apart by the same architect must be carbon copies. Nothing could be further from the truth. What exists at this complex is probably the finest original Ross combo in golfdom today.

The Mid Pines course occupies the lowlands portion of the two. The par 72 layout stretches thoughtfully through the pines and the wetlands. There is a decided economy to the design. The first and fifth greens meet where the second and sixth tees are located. The fifth and sixteenth greens congregate with the seventh and seventeenth tees. This would be considered busy in a design of today, but in the early 1920s this was de rigeur.

The premier holes at Mid Pines are the par three second, the short par four fourth, the murderous long three thirteenth, and the delectable finish—the doglegged seventeenth and the beautiful number eighteen.

Number four is a short par four hole that bends slightly from left to right and plays uphill to an elevated, truncated green. This is a hole that can be reached with a two iron and a sand wedge, but they better be a real good two iron and a real good sand wedge. Driving the ball any further than 200 yards on this hole will produce a nearly impossible second. The green is elevated and to get the ball close, the second shot must be hit in the air with a sufficient amount of spin. To describe the green and surroundings, it will suffice to say that I witnessed an accomplished four handicap hit his second on the green and spin it off the front. The pin was tucked on the right side on the upper plateau of the green. His chip was hit competently, yet a smidgen too hard. It rolled past the cup and off the green down into a little

OPPOSITE PAGE: VIEW FROM BEHIND A PROMINENT FAIRWAY BUNKER AT MID PINE'S HOLE NO. 17

swale. From here, he once again chipped ably but too forcefully and

THE BRIDGE LEADING TO THE GREEN AT
MID PINES'S HOLE NO. 2

returned to his original position in front of the green. His sixth shot placed the ball about two and a half feet from the pin. He was so bedeviled by this time that his putt never scented the hole. Simple hole, two iron, sand wedge, chip, chip, chip, putt, putt, seven. There were a few choice common phrases that emanated from his lips.

Number thirteen is one of the best long threes in the Ross arsenal: 230 yards from the back tee, a tree-lined fairway, and with bunkers left and right of the green that greet the player. The green is dual level, rising from the front right to the back left. The right side bunker is far enough away from the green to negate any real close attempts. There is not one flat spot on the green. This hole is the medal play contestant's worst nightmare. If the player misses the green, the possibility of five is quite high. If the player misses the green badly, the possibility of a triple, quadruple or worse is there as well.

Number seventeen is one of the finest doglegged four pars in existence. To gain real advantage on this hole, the player must play his tee shot over two perfectly placed bunkers that guard the right side of the fairway. Once this hazard is overcome, the player must figure out where to play his second shot. A ball placed on the wrong side of the green (which could be either side dependent on the pin position) can well cost the player three or even four putts.

Number eighteen at Mid Pines is a wonderful long par four, downhill off the tee and uphill

to the green. The putting green, the patio, and the old hotel frame the green. Plain and simple, it is a magnificent sight.

Pine Needles, the neighbor across the street, is in the uplands. That is, at least by comparison to Mid Pines. The feel of this course is totally different. The congestion of Mid Pines is replaced by the expanse of Pine Needles.

Pine Needles is one of those courses where the holes are so very good it is difficult to favor any one in particular. This said, I will try to describe two of the very best.

The fifth hole is my singular favorite Ross par three. It plays just over 210 yards from the back tee downhill to a green that slopes from back to front and left to right. It is really an offset affair that demands real accuracy off the tee. If the tee shot is left, right or long, par is pretty much out of the question. There is a bunker to the left that will catch errant shots. Although the bunker is fair, the shot that must be hit from it is really difficult as the green goes away from the player. The two short bunkers are far enough away from the green to cause similar problems, while the distance from the flag and the slope of the green negates sure success. Right of the green and long leaves angles that are nearly impossible to negotiate. The green itself is sloped, yet subtle. Two putts from past twenty feet is an accomplishment.

The seventeenth (formerly the finishing hole when the course was first opened) is another doglegged affair with a crucial bunker at the inside of the leg. The hole plays right to left, with the dogleg appearing about 195 yards from the tee. There is considerable *OPPOSITE PAGE:* THE MID PINES HOTEL

fairway straightaway off the tee, although the pines begin about 225 from the tee. If the tee shot is hit straightaway, however, the second will exceed 220 yards. Two-hundred-and-twenty yards down a bunkered alley to a medium-sized green—with out of bounds left and right—is not what one wants to face in search of par.

The tee shot must be played over the corner bunker. A pull or hook will catch the pines that block the left side. If the player is skilled enough to gain the fairway, he will have a long iron (three to five) into the green. To get to the green it is imperative to negotiate the short bunker left and the greenside bunker to the right. This is simply one of the most righteous par fours in the business.

Pine Needles and Mid Pines are two real gems. They provide thirty-six interesting, sculpted golf holes that have withstood the test of time for over 70 years. Either or both courses could be played daily by golfers of any level, and the enjoyment would increase with each play.

Perhaps the most alluring quality of these two venues is the family atmosphere engendered by the "First Lady of Golf," Peggy Kirk Bell. Her easy and friendly demeanor pervades the entire experience. Guests at the Mid Pines Hotel and the Pine Needles Lodge are encouraged to be part of the family, the Ross family, the Bell family, and the greater family of all real golfers.

COURSES FEATURING THE ARCHITECTURE
OF DONALD J. ROSS

SAGAMORE CLUBHOUSE

WATERBURY CLUBHOUSE

WORCESTER 4

POINT JUDITH 1

ALABAMA

COUNTRY CLUB OF BIRMINGHAM, BIRMINGHAM	1927
COUNTRY CLUB OF MOBILE, MOBILE	1928
MOUNTAIN BROOK CLUB, BIRMINGHAM	1929

CALIFORNIA

PENINSULA GOLF CLUB, SAN MATEO	1923

COLORADO

BROADMOOR GOLF CLUB, COLORADO SPRINGS	1918
LAKEWOOD GOLF CLUB, LAKEWOOD	1916
WELLSHIRE COUNTRY CLUB, DENVER	1924

CONNECTICUT

COUNTRY CLUB OF WATERBURY, WATERBURY	1926
GREENWICH COUNTRY CLUB, GREENWICH	1946
HARTFORD GOLF CLUB, WEST HARTFORD	1946
SHENNECOSSET COUNTRY CLUB, GROTON	1916
WAMPANOAG COUNTRY CLUB, WEST HARTFORD	1919

FLORIDA

BELLEAIR COUNTRY CLUB, BELLEAIR	1915
BENNEVIEW MIDO COUNTRY CLUB, BELLEAIR	1925
BILTMORE GOLF CLUB, CORAL GABLES	1925
BOBBY JONES MUNICIPAL GOLF COURSE, SARASOTA	1927
BOCA RATON GOLF CLUB, BOCA RATON	1925
BRENTWOOD GOLF CLUB, JACKSONVILLE	1922
DAYTONA BEACH GOLF AND COUNTRY CLUB, DAYTONA BEACH	1921
DELRAY BEACH MUNICIPAL GOLF COURSE, DELRAY BEACH	1925
DUNEDIN COUNTRY CLUB, DUNEDIN	1925
FLORIDA COUNTRY CLUB, JACKSONVILLE	1922
FORT GEORGE ISLAND GOLF CLUB, JACKSONVILLE	1922
FORT MYERS GOLF AND COUNTRY CLUB, FORT MYERS	1928
GULF STREAM GOLF CLUB, DELRAY BEACH	1923
HANDLEY GOLF CLUB, NEW SMYRNA BEACH	1922
HYDE PARK GOLF CLUB, JACKSONVILLE	1925
KEYSTONE GOLF AND COUNTRY CLUB, KEYSTONE HEIGHTS	1927
LAKE WALES COUNTRY CLUB, LAKE WALES	1925
MELBOURNE GOLF CLUB, MELBOURNE	1926
MIAMI COUNTRY CLUB, MIAMI	1919
NEW SMYRNA BEACH MUNICIPAL GOLF CLUB, NEW SMYRNA BEACH	1947
PALATKA MUNICIPAL GOLF COURSE, PALATKA	1925

PALM BEACH COUNTRY CLUB, PALM BEACH	1917
PALMA CEIA GOLF CLUB, TAMPA	1923
PALMA SOLA GOLF CLUB, GRADENTOWN	1924
PANAMA COUNTRY CLUB, LYNN HAVEN	1927
PINECREST ON LOTELA, AVON PARK	1926
PONCE DE LEON COUNTRY CLUB, ST. AUGUSTINE	1916
PUNTA GORDA COUNTRY CLUB, PUNTA GORDA	1927
COUNTRY CLUB OF ORLANDO, ORLANDO	1918
RIVIERA COUNTRY CLUB, CORAL GABLES	1924
SAN JOSE COUNTRY CLUB, JACKSONVILLE	1925
SARA BAY COUNTRY CLUB, SARASOTA	1925
SEMINOLE GOLF CLUB, NORTH PALM BEACH	1929
ST. AUGUSTINE LINKS, ST. AUGUSTINE	1916
TIMUQUANA COUNTRY CLUB, JACKSONVILLE	1923
UNIVERSITY OF FLORIDA GOLF CLUB, GAINESVILLE	1921

PLAINFIELD 17

POINT JUDITH 6

SCIOTO 10

GEORGIA	
ATHENS COUNTRY CLUB, ATHENS	1926
AUGUSTA COUNTRY CLUB, AUGUSTA	1927
BACON PARK GOLF CLUB, SAVANNAH	1926
BON-AIR-VANDERBILT, AUGUSTA	1925
BRUNSWICK COUNTRY CLUB, BRUNSWICK	1938
COUNTRY CLUB OF COLUMBUS, COLUMBUS	1915
EAST LAKE COUNTRY CLUB, ATLANTA	1915
FORREST HILLS GOLF CLUB, AUGUSTA	1926
HIGHLAND COUNTRY CLUB, LAGRANGE	1922
ROOSEVELT MEMORIAL GOLF CLUB, WARM SPRINGS	1926
SAFFOLDS GOLF COURSE, SAVANNAH	1926
SAVANNAH GOLF CLUB, SAVANNAH	1927
SHERATON SAVANNAH RESORT AND COUNTRY CLUB, SAVANNAH	1927
WALTHOUR GOLF COURSE, SAVANNAH	1928
WASHINGTON WILKES GOLF CLUB, WASHINGTON	1928

ILLINOIS	
BEVERLY COUNTRY CLUB, CHICAGO	1907
BOB O'LINK GOLF CLUB, HIGHLAND PARK	1916
CALUMET COUNTRY CLUB, HOMEWOOD	1917
EVANSTON GOLF CLUB, SKOKIE	1917
EXMOOR COUNTRY CLUB, HIGHLAND PARK	1914
HINSDALE GOLF CLUB, HINSDALE	1913
INDIAN HILL CLUB, WINNETKA	1914
NORTHMOOR COUNTRY CLUB, HIGHLAND PARK	1918
OAK PARK COUNTRY CLUB, OAK PARK	1916
OLD ELM CLUB, FORT SHERIDEN	1913
RAVISLOE COUNTRY CLUB, HOMEWOOD	1915
SKOKIE COUNTRY CLUB, GLENCOE	1915

INDIANA	
BROADMOOR COUNTRY CLUB, INDIANAPOLIS	1921
FAIRVIEW GOLF CLUB, FORT WAYNE	1927
FRENCH LICK GOLF COURSE, FRENCH LICK	1917

IOWA	
CEDAR RAPIDS COUNTRY CLUB, CEDAR RAPIDS	1915

KANSAS	
SHAWNEE COUNTRY CLUB, TOPEKA	1915

KENTUCKY	
IDLE HOUR COUNTRY CLUB, LEXINGTON	1924

MAINE	
AUGUSTA COUNTRY CLUB, MANCHESTER	1916
BIDDEFORD SACO COUNTRY CLUB, SACO	1921
CAPE NEDDICK COUNTRY CLUB, YORK	1919
LAKE KEZAR GOLF CLUB, LOWELL	1918
LUCERNE-IN-MAINE, BANGOR	1926
NORTHEAST HARBORS, NORTHEAST HARBORS	1922
PARADISE SPRINGS GOLF CLUB, PARADISE SPRINGS	1920
PENOBSCOT VALLEY COUNTRY CLUB, BANGOR	1923
POLAND SPRINGS COUNTRY CLUB, POLAND SPRINGS	1913
PORTLAND COUNTRY CLUB, FALMOUTH	1921
YORK GOLF & TENNIS CLUB, YORK HARBOR	1923

ARONOMINK CLUBHOUSE

HOLSTON HILLS 15   BRAE BURN 9

MARYLAND

BANNOCKBURN GOLF CLUB, GLEN ECHO	1924
CHEVY CHASE COUNTRY CLUB, CHEVY CHASE	1915
CONGRESSIONAL COUNTRY CLUB, BETHESDA	1930
INDIAN SPRING COUNTRY CLUB, LAUREL	1922
PRINCE GEORGES COUNTRY CLUB, LANDOVER	1921
SILVER SPRINGS GOLF CLUB, SILVER SPRINGS	1921

MASSACHUSETTS

BASS RIVER GOLF COURSE, YARMOUTH	1914
BELMONT COUNTRY CLUB, BELMONT	1918
BRAE BURN COUNTRY CLUB, WEST NEWTON	1912
CHARLES RIVER COUNTRY CLUB, NEWTON CENTRE	1921
COHASSE GOLF CLUB, SOUTHBRIDGE	1916
COHASSET GOLF CLUB, COHASSET	1922
CONCORD COUNTRY CLUB, CONCORD	1913
ELLINWOOD COUNTRY CLUB, ATHOL	1927
ESSEX COUNTY CLUB, MANCHESTER	1909
GEORGE WRIGHT MUNICIPAL GOLF COURSE, BOSTON	1931
GREENOCK COUNTRY CLUB, LEE	1927
HYANNISPORT CLUB, HYANNISPORT	1936
KERNWOOD COUNTRY CLUB, SALEM	1914

LONGMEADOW COUNTRY CLUB	1921
LUDLOW COUNTRY CLUB, LUDLOW	1920
COUNTRY CLUB OF NEW BEDFORD, DARTMOUTH	1924
NANTUCKET GOLF CLUB, NANTUCKET	1917
NEWTON COMMONWEALTH, NEWTON	1921
NORTH ANDOVER COUNTRY CLUB, NORTH ANDOVER	1920
OAK HILL COUNTRY CLUB, FITCHBURG	1921
OAKLEY COUNTRY CLUB, WATERTOWN	1900
THE ORCHARDS COUNTRY CLUB, SOUTH HADLEY	1922
OYSTER HARBORS CLUB, OSTERVILLE	1927
COUNTRY CLUB OF PITTSFIELD, PITTSFIELD	1921
PLYMOUTH COUNTRY CLUB, PLYMOUTH	1927
POCASSET GOLF CLUB, POCASSET	1916
PONKAPOAG GOLF CLUB, CANTON	1931
SALEM COUNTRY CLUB, PEABODY	1925
SANDY BURR COUNTRY CLUB, WAYLAND	1924
SPRINGFIELD COUNTRY CLUB, SPRINGFIELD	1924
TATNUCK COUNTRY CLUB, WORCESTER	1930
TEKOA COUNTRY CLUB, WESTFIELD	1923
TOYTOWN TAVERN GOLF CLUB, WINCHENDON	1924
VESPER COUNTRY CLUB, TYNGSBORO	1919
WACHUSSETT COUNTRY CLUB, WEST BOYLSTON	1927

WALTHAM COUNTRY CLUB, WALTHAM	1921
WELLESLEY COUNTRY CLUB, WELLESLEY	1910
WESTON GOLF CLUB, WESTON	1916
WHALING CITY COUNTRY CLUB, NEW BEDFORD	1920
WHITINSVILLE GOLF CLUB, WHITINSVILLE	1923
WIANNO GOLF CLUB, OSTERVILLE	1920
WINCHESTER COUNTRY CLUB, WINCHESTER	1903
WOODLAND GOLF CLUB, AUBURNDALE	1927
WORCESTER COUNTRY CLUB, WORCESTER	1913
WYCKOFF PARK GOLF CLUB, HOLYOKE	1923

MICHIGAN

BARTON HILLS COUNTRY CLUB, ANN ARBOR	1920
BLOOMFIELD HILLS COUNTRY CLUB, BLOOMFIELD HILLS	1936
BRIGHTMOOR COUNTRY CLUB, DEARBORN	1925
DETROIT GOLF CLUB, DETROIT	1916
ELK GRAND RAPIDS GOLF CLUB, ELK RAPIDS	1923
FRANKLIN HILLS COUNTRY CLUB, FRANKLIN	1926
FRED WARDELL ESTATE GOLF CLUB, DETROIT	1920
GROSSE ILE GOLF AND COUNTRY CLUB, GROSSE ILE	1919
HIGHLANDS PARK GOLF CLUB, GRAND RAPIDS	1922
KENT COUNTRY CLUB, GRAND RAPIDS	1921

PLAINFIELD 7

WORCESTER CLUBHOUSE   THE ORCHARDS 12

MONROE GOLF AND COUNTRY CLUB, MONROE	1919	NEW HAMPSHIRE		MOUNTAIN RIDGE COUNTRY CLUB, WEST CALDWELL	1929
MUSKEGON COUNTRY CLUB, MUSKEGON	1911	BALD PEAK COLONY CLUB, MOULTONBORO	1922	PLAINFIELD COUNTRY CLUB, PLAINFIELD	1916
OAKLAND HILLS COUNTRY CLUB, BIRMINGHAM	1917	BALSAM'S GR & GOLF CLUB, DIXVILLE NOTCH	1912	RIDGEWOOD COUNTRY CLUB, RIDGEWOOD	1916
RACKHAM MUNICIPAL GOLF COURSE, HUNTINGTON WOODS	1923	BETHLEHEM COUNTRY CLUB, BETHLEHEM	1910	RIVERTON COUNTRY CLUB, RIVERTON	1916
ROGELL GOLF CLUB, DETROIT	1921	CARTER COUNTRY CLUB, LEBANON	1923	SEAVIEW COUNTRY CLUB, ABSECON	1915
SHADOW RIDGE COUNTRY CLUB, IONIA	1916	KINGSWOOD COUNTRY CLUB, WOLFEBORO	1926		
ST. CLAIR RIVER COUNTRY CLUB, ST. CLAIR	1923	LAKE SUNAPEE COUNTRY CLUB, NEW LONDON	1927	NEW YORK	
WARREN VALLEY GOLF CLUB, DEARBORN	1927	LAKE TARLETON PIKE, PIKE	1916	BELLEVUE COUNTRY CLUB, SYRACUSE	1914
WESTERN GOLF AND COUNTRY CLUB, REDFORD	1926	MANCHESTER COUNTRY CLUB, MANCHESTER	1921	BROOK LEA COUNTRY CLUB, ROCHESTER	1925
		MAPLEWOOD COUNTRY CLUB, BETHLEHEM	1914	COUNTRY CLUB OF BUFFALO, WILLIAMSVILLE	1923
MINNESOTA		MT. WASHINGTON GOLF CLUB, BRETTON WOODS	1915	CHAPPAQUA GOLF CLUB, MT. KISCO	1929
INTERLACHEN COUNTRY CLUB, EDINA	1919	TORY PINES RESORT, FRANCESTOWN	1929	CHAUTAUQUA GOLF CLUB, CHAUTAUQUA	1921
MINIKAHDA CLUB, MINNEAPOLIS	1917	WENTWORTH-BY-THE-SEA, PORTSMOUTH	1910	ELMSFORD COUNTRY CLUB, ELMSFORD	1919
MINNEAPOLIS GOLF CLUB, MINNEAPOLIS	1920			FAIRVIEW COUNTRY CLUB, ELMSFORD	1920
NORTHLAND COUNTRY CLUB, DULUTH	1927	NEW JERSEY		FOX HILLS GOLF CLUB, STATEN ISLAND	1928
WHITE BEAR YACHT CLUB, WHITE BEAR LAKE	1912	CRESTMONT COUNTRY CLUB, WEST ORANGE	1921	GLENS FALLS COUNTRY CLUB, GLENS FALLS	1921
WOODHILL COUNTRY CLUB, WAYZATA	1916	ECHO LAKE COUNTRY CLUB, WESTFIELD	1919	HUDSON RIVER GOLF CLUB, YONKERS	1916
		ESSEX COUNTY COUNTRY CLUB, WEST ORANGE	1924	IRONDEQUOIT COUNTRY CLUB, ROCHESTER	1916
MISSOURI		HOMESTEAD COUNTRY CLUB, SPRING LAKE	1920	MARK TWAIN GOLF COURSE, ELMIRA	1937
HILLCREST COUNTRY CLUB, KANSAS CITY	1917	KNICKERBOCKER COUNTRY CLUB, TENAFLY	1915	MONROE GOLF CLUB, PITTSFORD	1923
MIDLAND VALLEY COUNTRY CLUB, OVERLAND	1919	LONE PINE GOLF CLUB, VERONA	1925	OAK HILL COUNTRY CLUB, ROCHESTER	1923
		MONTCLAIR GOLF CLUB, MONTCLAIR	1919		

SALEM 13

ESSEX 18   PINEHURST CLUBHOUSE

RIP VAN WINKLE COUNTRY CLUB, PALENVILLE	1919	CHARLOTTE COUNTRY CLUB, CHARLOTTE	1923	PINEHURST COUNTRY CLUB NO. 5, PINEHURST	1927
COUNTRY CLUB OF ROCHESTER, ROCHESTER	1913	FORSYTH COUNTRY CLUB, WINSTON SALEM	1920	RALEIGH COUNTRY CLUB, RALEIGH	1947
THE SAGAMORE RESORT & GOLF CLUB, LAKE GEORGE	1928	GREENSBORO COUNTRY CLUB, GREENSBORO	1911	RICHMOND PINES COUNTRY CLUB, ROCKINGHAM	1926
SIWANOY GOLF CLUB, BRONXVILLE	1914	GROVE PARK INN, ASHEVILLE	1924	ROARING GAP GOLF CLUB, ROARING GAP	1925
TEUGEGA COUNTRY CLUB, ROME	1920	HENDERSONVILLE COUNTRY CLUB, HENDERSONVILLE	1925	COUNTRY CLUB OF SALISBURY, SALISBURY	1927
THENDARA GOLF CLUB, THENDARA	1921	HIGHLAND COUNTRY CLUB, FAYETTEVILLE	1945	SEDGEFIELD COUNTRY CLUB, GREENSBORO	1924
TUPPER LAKE COUNTRY CLUB, TUPPER LAKE	1915	HIGHLANDS COUNTRY CLUB, HIGHLANDS	1926	SOUTHERN PINES COUNTRY CLUB, SOUTHERN PINES	1923
WHIPPOORWILL COUNTRY CLUB, ARMONK	1925	HOPE VALLEY COUNTRY CLUB, DURHAM	1926	STRYKER GOLF CLUB, FAYETTEVILLE	1946
WYKAGYL COUNTRY CLUB, NEW ROCHELLE	1920	LENOIR GOLF CLUB, LENOIR	1928	TRYON COUNTRY CLUB, TRYON	1916
		LINVILLE GOLF CLUB, LINVILLE	1924	WILMINGTON MUNICIPAL GOLF COURSE, WILMINGTON	1925
		MID PINES CLUB, SOUTHERN PINES	1921	WAYNESVILLE COUNTRY CLUB, WAYNESVILLE	1924
NORTH CAROLINA		MIMOSA HILLS GOLF CLUB, MORGANTOWN	1928		
ALAMANCE COUNTRY CLUB, BURLINGTON	1946	MONROE GOLF CLUB, MONROE	1927		
ASHEVILLE COUNTRY CLUB, ASHEVILLE	1928	MOORE PARK GOLF CLUB, MOORESVILLE	1948	OHIO	
BENVENUE COUNTRY CLUB, ROCKY MOUNT	1922	MYERS PARK COUNTRY CLUB, CHARLOTTE	1930	ACACIA COUNTRY CLUB, LYNDHURST	1920
BILTMORE FOREST COUNTRY CLUB, ASHEVILLE	1921	OVERHILLS	1910	ALADDIN COUNTRY CLUB, COLUMBUS	1921
BLOWING ROCK COUNTRY CLUB, BLOWING ROCK	1922	PENNROSE PARK COUNTRY CLUB, REIDSVILLE	1945	ATHENS COUNTRY CLUB, ATHENS	1921
BUNCOMBE COUNTY GOLF CLUB, ASHEVILLE	1927	PINE NEEDLES COUNTRY CLUB, SOUTHERN PINES	1927	BROOKSIDE COUNTRY CLUB, CANTON	1922
CAPE FEAR COUNTRY CLUB, WILMINGTON	1924	PINEHURST COUNTRY CLUB NO. 1, PINEHURST	1900	COLUMBUS COUNTRY CLUB, COLUMBUS	1914
CAROLINA GOLF AND COUNTRY CLUB, CHARLOTTE	1928	PINEHURST COUNTRY CLUB NO. 2, PINEHURST	1901	CONGRESS LAKE CLUB, HARTVILLE	1929
CAROLINA PINES GOLF CLUB, RALEIGH	1932	PINEHURST COUNTRY CLUB NO. 3, PINEHURST	1907	DAYTON GOLF & COUNTRY CLUB, DAYTON	1919
CATAWBA COUNTRY CLUB, HICKORY	1946	PINEHURST COUNTRY CLUB NO. 4, PINEHURST	1912	DELAWARE GOLF CLUB, DELAWARE	1922
				ELKS COUNTRY CLUB OF COLUMBUS, COLUMBUS	1921

POINT JUDITH 10

SCIOTO 1   INVERNESS 15

GRANVILLE GOLF CLUB, GRANVILLE	1924
HAMILTON ELKS COUNTRY CLUB, HAMILTON	1925
HAWTHORNE VALLEY COUNTRY CLUB, SOLON	1926
HYDE PARK GOLF AND COUNTRY CLUB, CINCINNATI	1927
INVERNESS CLUB, TOLEDO	1920
LANCASTER COUNTRY CLUB, LANCASTER	1928
MAKETEWAH COUNTRY CLUB, CINCINNATI	1919
MANAKIKI GOLF CLUB, WILLOUGHBY	1928
MIAMI SHORES GOLF CLUB, TROY	1926
MILL CREEK PARK GOLF CLUB, YOUNGSTOWN	1928
MOHAWK GOLF CLUB, TIFFIN	1917
OAKWOOD COUNTRY CLUB, CLEVELAND	1915
PIQUA COUNTRY CLUB, PIQUA	1920
PORTSMITH ELKS COUNTRY CLUB, MCDERMOTT	1920
SCIOTO COUNTRY CLUB, COLUMBUS	1916
SHAKER HEIGHTS COUNTRY CLUB, SHAKER HEIGHTS	1913
SPRINGFIELD COUNTRY CLUB, SPRINGFIELD	1921
WESTBROOK COUNTRY CLUB, MANSFIELD	1920
WILLOWICK COUNTRY CLUB, CLEVELAND	1917
WYANDOT MUNICIPAL GOLF COURSE, WORTHINGTON	1922
YOUNGSTOWN COUNTRY CLUB, YOUNGSTOWN	1921
ZANEVILLE COUNTRY CLUB, ZANEVILLE	1932

PENNSYLVANIA

ALLEGHENY COUNTRY CLUB, SEWICKLEY	1923
ARONIMINK GOLF CLUB, NEWTOWN SQUARE	1928
BEDFORD SPRINGS HOTEL, BEDFORD SPRINGS	1924
BUCK HILL GOLF CLUB, BUCK HILL FALLS	1922
CEDARBROOK COUNTRY CLUB, BLUE BELL	1921
EDGEWOOD COUNTRY CLUB, PITTSBURGH	1921
ELKVIEW GOLF CLUB, CARBONDALE	1925
GREEN OAKS, VERONA	1921
GULPH MILLS GOLF CLUB, KING OF PRUSSIA	1919
KAHKWA CLUB, ERIE	1915
KENNETT SQUARE GOLF & COUNTRY CLUB, KENNETT SQUARE	1923
LEWISTOWN COUNTRY CLUB, LEWISTOWN	1945
LULU TEMPLE COUNTRY CLUB, NORTH HILLS	1912
OVERBROOK GOLF CLUB, PHILADELPHIA	1922
PHILADELPHIA CKC, PHILADELPHIA	1914
POCONO MANOR GOLF COURSE, WHITE HAVEN	1919
ROLLING ROCK CLUB, LIGONIER	1916
SCHUYLKILL COUNTRY CLUB, POTTSVILLE	1945
SILVERCREEK COUNTRY CLUB, HELLERTOWN	1947
ST. DAVIDS GOLF CLUB, WAYNE	1927
SUNNYBROOK COUNTRY CLUB, FLOURTOWN	1921

TORRESDALE FRANKFORD COUNTRY CLUB, PHILADELPHIA	1919
TUMBLEBROOK COUNTRY CLUB, COOPERS BROOK	1931
WHITEMARSH VALLEY COUNTRY CLUB, LAFAYETTE HILL	1930
COUNTRY CLUB OF YORK, YORK	1927

RHODE ISLAND

AGAWAM HUNT CLUB, RUMFORD	1911
METACOMET COUNTRY CLUB, EAST PROVIDENCE	1921
MISQUAMICUT CLUB, WESTERLY	1923
NEWPORT COUNTRY CLUB, NEWPORT	1915
POINT JUDITH COUNTRY CLUB, NARRAGANSETT	1927
RHODE ISLAND COUNTRY CLUB, WEST BARRINGTON	1911
SAKONNET GOLF CLUB, LITTLE COMPTON	1921
TRIGGS MEMORIAL GOLF CLUB, NORTH PROVIDENCE	1930
WANNAMOISETT COUNTRY CLUB, RUMFORD	1914
WARWICK COUNTRY CLUB, WARWICK NECK	1924
WINNAPAUG GOLF CLUB, WESTERLY	1921

ESSEX LOCKER ROOM HOLSTON HILLS INSIGNIA HOLSTON HILLS 15 ESSEX CLUBHOUSE

HOLSTON HILLS 15

SOUTH CAROLINA	
CAMDEN COUNTRY CLUB, CAMDEN	1939
FORT MILL GOLF CLUB, FORT MILL	1947
LANCASTER GOLF CLUB, LANCASTER	1935

TENNESSEE	
BELLE MEADE COUNTRY CLUB, NASHVILLE	1921
BRAINERD GOLF & COUNTRY CLUB, CHATTANOOGA	1925
CHATTANOOGA COUNTRY CLUB, CHATTANOOGA	1920
CHEROKEE COUNTRY CLUB, KNOXVILLE	1910
HOLSTON HILLS COUNTRY CLUB, KNOXVILLE	1928
MEMPHIS COUNTRY CLUB, MEMPHIS	1910
RICHLAND COUNTRY CLUB, NASHVILLE	1920
RIDGEFIELDS COUNTRY CLUB, KINGSPORT	1947
TATE SPRINGS HOTEL & COUNTRY CLUB, BEAN STATION	1924

TEXAS	
GALVESTON COUNTRY CLUB, GALVESTON	1921
RIVER OAKS COUNTRY CLUB, HOUSTON	1924
SUNSET GROVE COUNTRY CLUB, ORANGE	1923

VERMONT	
BURLINGTON COUNTRY CLUB, BURLINGTON	1930
WOODSTOCK COUNTRY CLUB, WOODSTOCK	1938

VIRGINIA	
BELMONT PARK, RICHMOND	1940
HAMPTON GOLF CLUB, HAMPTON	1921
THE HOMESTEAD HOTEL & GOLF CLUB, HOT SPRINGS	1912
JEFFERSON-LAKESIDE COUNTRY CLUB, RICHMOND	1921
KINDERTON COUNTRY CLUB, CLARKSVILLE	1947
COUNTRY CLUB OF PETERSBURG, PETERSBURG	1922
SEWELLS PT. GOLF CLUB, NORFOLK	1927
COUNTRY CLUB OF VIRGINIA, RICHMOND	1921
WASHINGTON GOLF AND COUNTRY CLUB, ARLINGTON	1915
WESTWOOD GOLF CLUB, VIENNA	1926
WOODBURY FOREST GOLF CLUB, WOODBURY FOREST	1910

WISCONSIN	
KENOSHA COUNTRY CLUB, KENOSHA	1922
OCONOMOWOC COUNTRY CLUB, OCONOMOWOC	1915

CANADA	
ALGONQUIN HOTEL AND GOLF CLUB, ST. ANDREWS, NEW BRUNSWICK	1927
BANFF HOTEL GOLF CLUB, BANFF SPRINGS	1912
BRIGHTWOOD GOLF AND COUNTRY CLUB, DARTMOUTH, NOVA SCOTIA	1934
ESSEX GOLF AND COUNTRY CLUB, LASALLE, ONTARIO	1929
ELMHURST GOLF LINKS, WINNIPEG, MANITOBA	1923
LIVERPOOL GOLF CLUB, HUNTS POINT, NOVA SCOTIA	1929
PINE RIDGE COUNTRY CLUB, WINNIPEG, MANITOBA	1919
RIVERSIDE GOLF AND COUNTRY CLUB, NEW BRUNSWICK	1937
ROSEDALE GOLF CLUB, TORONTO, ONTARIO	1919
ROSELAND GOLF AND COUNTRY CLUB, WINDSOR, ONTARIO	1921
ST. CHARLES COUNTRY CLUB, WINNIPEG, MANITOBA	1920

CUBA	
COUNTRY CLUB OF HAVANA, HAVANA	1911
HAVANA BILTMORE GOLF CLUB, HAVANA	1927

ALABAMA / COUNTRY CLUB OF BIRMINGHAM, BIRMINGHAM, 1927 / COUNTRY CLUB OF MOBILE, MOBILE, 1928 / MOUNTAIN BROOK CLUB, BIRMINGHAM, 1929 / *CALIFORNIA* / PENINSULA GOLF CLUB, SAN MATEO, 1923 / *COLORADO* / BROADMOOR GOLF CLUB, COLORADO SPRINGS, 1918 / LAKEWOOD GOLF CLUB, LAKEWOOD, 1916 / WELLSHIRE COUNTRY CLUB, DENVER, 1924 / *CONNECTICUT* / COUNTRY CLUB OF WATERBURY, WATERBURY, 1926 / GREENWICH COUNTRY CLUB, GREENWICH, 1946 / HARTFORD GOLF CLUB, WEST HARTFORD, 1946 / SHENNECOSSET COUNTRY CLUB, GROTON, 1916 / WAMPANOAG COUNTRY CLUB, WEST HARTFORD, 1919 / *FLORIDA* / BELLEAIR COUNTRY CLUB, BELLEAIR, 1915 / BENNEVIEW MIDO COUNTRY CLUB, BELLEAIR, 1925 / BILTMORE GOLF CLUB, CORAL GABLES, 1925 / BOBBY JONES MUNICIPAL GOLF COURSE, SARASOTA, 1927 / BOCA RATON GOLF CLUB, BOCA RATON, 1925 / BRENTWOOD GOLF CLUB, JACKSONVILLE, 1922 / DAYTONA BEACH GOLF AND COUNTRY CLUB, DAYTONA BEACH, 1921 / DELRAY BEACH MUNICIPAL GOLF COURSE, DELRAY BEACH, 1925 / DUNEDIN COUNTRY CLUB, DUNEDIN, 1925 / FLORIDA COUNTRY CLUB, JACKSONVILLE, 1922 / FORT GEORGE ISLAND GOLF CLUB, JACKSONVILLE, 1922 / FORT MYERS GOLF AND COUNTRY CLUB, FORT MYERS, 1928 / GULF STREAM GOLF CLUB, DELRAY BEACH, 1923 / HANDLEY GOLF CLUB, NEW SMYRNA BEACH, 1922 / HYDE PARK GOLF CLUB, JACKSONVILLE, 1925 / KEYSTONE GOLF AND COUNTRY CLUB, KEYSTONE HEIGHTS, 1927 / LAKE WALES COUNTRY CLUB, LAKE WALES, 1925 / MELBOURNE GOLF CLUB, MELBOURNE, 1926 / MIAMI COUNTRY CLUB, MIAMI, 1919 / NEW SMYRNA BEACH MUNICIPAL GOLF CLUB, NEW SMYRNA BEACH, 1947 / PALATKA MUNICIPAL GOLF COURSE, PALATKA, 1925 / PALM BEACH COUNTRY CLUB, PALM BEACH, 1917 / PALMA CEIA GOLF CLUB, TAMPA, 1923 / PALMA SOLA GOLF CLUB, GRADENTOWN, 1924 / PANAMA COUNTRY CLUB, LYNN HAVEN, 1927 / PINECREST ON LOTELA, AVON PARK, 1926 / PONCE DE LEON COUNTRY CLUB, ST. AUGUSTINE, 1916 / PUNTA GORDA COUNTRY CLUB, PUNTA GORDA, 1927 / COUNTRY CLUB OF ORLANDO, ORLANDO, 1918 / RIVIERA COUNTRY CLUB, CORAL GABLES, 1924 / SAN JOSE COUNTRY CLUB, JACKSONVILLE, 1925 / SARA BAY COUNTRY CLUB, SARASOTA, 1925 / SEMINOLE GOLF CLUB, NORTH PALM BEACH, 1929 / ST. AUGUSTINE LINKS, ST. AUGUSTINE, 1916 / TIMUQUANA COUNTRY CLUB, JACKSONVILLE, 1923 / UNIVERSITY OF FLORIDA GOLF CLUB, GAINESVILLE, 1921 / *GEORGIA* / ATHENS COUNTRY CLUB, ATHENS, 1926 / AUGUSTA COUNTRY CLUB, AUGUSTA, 1927 / BACON PARK GOLF CLUB, SAVANNAH, 1926 / BON-AIR-VANDERBILT, AUGUSTA, 1925 / BRUNSWICK COUNTRY CLUB, BRUNSWICK, 1938 / COUNTRY CLUB OF COLUMBUS, COLUMBUS, 1915 / EAST LAKE COUNTRY CLUB, ATLANTA, 1915 / FORREST HILLS GOLF CLUB, AUGUSTA, 1926 / HIGHLAND COUNTRY CLUB, LAGRANGE, 1922 / ROOSEVELT MEMORIAL GOLF CLUB, WARM SPRINGS, 1926 / SAFFOLDS GOLF COURSE, SAVANNAH, 1926 / SAVANNAH GOLF CLUB, SAVANNAH, 1927 / SHERATON SAVANNAH RESORT AND COUNTRY CLUB, SAVANNAH, 1927 / WALTHOUR GOLF COURSE, SAVANNAH, 1928 / WASHINGTON WILKES GOLF CLUB, WASHINGTON, 1928 / *ILLINOIS* / BEVERLY COUNTRY CLUB, CHICAGO, 1907 / BOB O'LINK GOLF CLUB, HIGHLAND PARK, 1916 / CALUMET COUNTRY CLUB, HOMEWOOD, 1917 / EVANSTON GOLF CLUB, SKOKIE, 1917 / EXMOOR COUNTRY CLUB, HIGHLAND PARK, 1914 / HINSDALE GOLF CLUB, HINSDALE, 1913 / INDIAN HILL CLUB, WINNETKA, 1914 / NORTHMOOR COUNTRY CLUB, HIGHLAND PARK, 1918 / OAK PARK COUNTRY CLUB, OAK PARK, 1916 / OLD ELM CLUB, FORT SHERIDEN, 1913 / RAVISLOE COUNTRY CLUB, HOMEWOOD, 1915 / SKOKIE COUNTRY CLUB, GLENCOE, 1915 / *INDIANA* / BROADMOOR COUNTRY CLUB, INDIANAPOLIS, 1921 / FAIRVIEW GOLF CLUB, FORT WAYNE, 1927 / FRENCH LICK GOLF COURSE, FRENCH LICK, 1917 / *IOWA* / CEDAR RAPIDS COUNTRY CLUB, CEDAR RAPIDS, 1915 / KANSAS / SHAWNEE COUNTRY CLUB, TOPEKA, 1915 / *KENTUCKY* / IDLE HOUR COUNTRY CLUB, LEXINGTON, 1924 / *MAINE* / AUGUSTA COUNTRY CLUB, MANCHESTER, 1916 / BIDDEFORD SACO COUNTRY CLUB, SACO, 1921 / CAPE NEDDICK COUNTRY CLUB, YORK, 1919 / LAKE KEZAR GOLF CLUB, LOWELL, 1918 / LUCERNE-IN-MAINE, BANGOR, 1926 / NORTHEAST HARBORS, NORTHEAST HARBORS, 1922 / PARADISE SPRINGS GOLF CLUB, PARADISE SPRINGS, 1920 / PENOBSCOT VALLEY COUNTRY CLUB, BANGOR, 1923 / POLAND SPRINGS COUNTRY CLUB, POLAND SPRINGS, 1913 / PORTLAND COUNTRY CLUB, FALMOUTH, 1921 / YORK GOLF & TENNIS CLUB, YORK HARBOR, 1923 / *MARYLAND* / BANNOCKBURN GOLF CLUB, GLEN ECHO, 1924 / CHEVY CHASE COUNTRY CLUB, CHEVY CHASE, 1915 / CONGRESSIONAL COUNTRY CLUB, BETHESDA, 1930 / INDIAN SPRING COUNTRY CLUB, LAUREL, 1922 / PRINCE GEORGES COUNTRY CLUB, LANDOVER, 1921 / SILVER SPRINGS GOLF CLUB, SILVER SPRINGS, 1921 / *MASSACHUSETTS* / BASS RIVER GOLF COURSE, YARMOUTH, 1914 / BELMONT COUNTRY CLUB, BELMONT, 1918 / BRAE BURN COUNTRY CLUB, WEST NEWTON, 1912 / CHARLES RIVER COUNTRY CLUB, NEWTON CENTRE, 1921 / COHASSE GOLF CLUB, SOUTHBRIDGE, 1916 / COHASSET GOLF CLUB, COHASSET, 1922 / CONCORD COUNTRY CLUB, CONCORD, 1913 / ELLINWOOD COUNTRY CLUB, ATHOL, 1927 / ESSEX COUNTY CLUB, MANCHESTER, 1909 / GEORGE WRIGHT MUNICIPAL GOLF COURSE, BOSTON, 1931 / GREENOCK COUNTRY CLUB, LEE, 1927 / HYANNISPORT CLUB, HYANNISPORT, 1936 / KERNWOOD COUNTRY CLUB, SALEM, 1914 / LONGMEADOW COUNTRY CLUB, 1921 / LUDLOW COUNTRY CLUB, LUDLOW, 1920 / COUNTRY CLUB OF NEW BEDFORD, DARTMOUTH, 1924 / NANTUCKET GOLF CLUB, NANTUCKET, 1917 / NEWTON COMMONWEALTH, NEWTON, 1921 / NORTH ANDOVER COUNTRY CLUB, NORTH ANDOVER, 1920 / OAK HILL COUNTRY CLUB, FITCHBURG, 1921 / OAKLEY COUNTRY CLUB, WATERTOWN, 1900 / THE ORCHARDS COUNTRY CLUB, SOUTH HADLEY, 1922 / OYSTER HARBORS CLUB, OSTERVILLE, 1927 / COUNTRY

CLUB OF PITTSFIELD, PITTSFIELD, 1921 / PLYMOUTH COUNTRY CLUB, PLYMOUTH, 1927 / POCASSET GOLF CLUB, POCASSET, 1916 / PONKAPOAG GOLF CLUB, CAN
COUNTRY CLUB, WORCESTER, 1930 / TEKOA COUNTRY CLUB, WESTFIELD, 1923 / TOYTOWN TAVERN GOLF CLUB, WINCHENDON, 1924 / VESPER COUNTRY CLUB, TY
WESTON GOLF CLUB, WESTON, 1916 / WHALING CITY COUNTRY CLUB, NEW BEDFORD, 1920 / WHITINSVILLE GOLF CLUB, WHITINSVILLE, 1923 / WIANNO GOLF CLUB
/ WYCKOFF PARK GOLF CLUB, HOLYOKE, 1923 / *MICHIGAN* / BARTON HILLS COUNTRY CLUB, ANN ARBOR, 1920 / BLOOMFIELD HILLS COUNTRY CLUB, BLOOMFIELD
HILLS COUNTRY CLUB, FRANKLIN, 1926 / FRED WARDELL ESTATE GOLF CLUB, DETROIT, 1920 / GROSSE ILE GOLF AND COUNTRY CLUB, GROSSE ILE, 1919 / HIGHLA
CLUB, MUSKEGON, 1911 / OAKLAND HILLS COUNTRY CLUB, BIRMINGHAM, 1917 / RACKHAM MUNICIPAL GOLF COURSE, HUNTINGTON WOODS, 1923 / ROGELL GOL
1927 / WESTERN GOLF AND COUNTRY CLUB, REDFORD, 1926 / *MINNESOTA* / INTERLACHEN COUNTRY CLUB, EDINA, 1919 / MINIKAHDA CLUB, MINNEAPOLIS, 1917 /
CLUB, WAYZATA, 1916 / *MISSOURI* / HILLCREST COUNTRY CLUB, KANSAS CITY, 1917 / MIDLAND VALLEY COUNTRY CLUB, OVERLAND, 1919 / *NEW HAMPSHIRE* / BAL
CLUB, LEBANON, 1923 / KINGSWOOD COUNTRY CLUB, WOLFEBORO, 1926 / LAKE SUNAPEE COUNTRY CLUB, NEW LONDON, 1927 / LAKE TARLETON PIKE, PIKE, 191
PINES RESORT, FRANCESTOWN, 1929 / WENTWORTH-BY-THE-SEA, PORTSMOUTH, 1910 / *NEW JERSEY* / CRESTMONT COUNTRY CLUB, WEST ORANGE, 1921 / ECHO
COUNTRY CLUB, TENAFLY, 1915 / LONE PINE GOLF CLUB, VERONA, 1925 / MONTCLAIR GOLF CLUB, MONTCLAIR, 1919 / MOUNTAIN RIDGE COUNTRY CLUB, WEST CAL
COUNTRY CLUB, ABSECON, 1915 / *NEW YORK* / BELLEVUE COUNTRY CLUB, SYRACUSE, 1914 / BROOK LEA COUNTRY CLUB, ROCHESTER, 1925 / COUNTRY CLUB OF
1919 / FAIRVIEW COUNTRY CLUB, ELMSFORD, 1920 / FOX HILLS GOLF CLUB, STATEN ISLAND, 1928 / GLENS FALLS COUNTRY CLUB, GLENS FALLS, 1921 / HUDSON
1923 / OAK HILL COUNTRY CLUB, ROCHESTER, 1923 / RIP VAN WINKLE COUNTRY CLUB, PALENVILLE, 1919 / COUNTRY CLUB OF ROCHESTER, ROCHESTER, 1913 / T
THENDARA, 1921 / TUPPER LAKE COUNTRY CLUB, TUPPER LAKE, 1915 / WHIPPOORWILL COUNTRY CLUB, ARMONK, 1925 / WYKAGYL COUNTRY CLUB, NEW ROCHELLE
1922 / BILTMORE FOREST COUNTRY CLUB, ASHEVILLE, 1921 / BLOWING ROCK COUNTRY CLUB, BLOWING ROCK, 1922 / BUNCOMBE COUNTY GOLF CLUB, ASHEVIL
CATAWBA COUNTRY CLUB, HICKORY, 1946 / CHARLOTTE COUNTRY CLUB, CHARLOTTE, 1923 / FORSYTH COUNTRY CLUB, WINSTON SALEM, 1920 / GREENSBORO C
FAYETTEVILLE, 1945 / HIGHLANDS COUNTRY CLUB, HIGHLANDS, 1926 / HOPE VALLEY COUNTRY CLUB, DURHAM, 1926 / LENOIR GOLF CLUB, LENOIR, 1928 / LINVI
MOORE PARK GOLF CLUB, MOORESVILLE, 1948 / MYERS PARK COUNTRY CLUB, CHARLOTTE, 1930 / OVERHILLS, 1910 / PENNROSE PARK COUNTRY CLUB, REIDSVILLE
1901 / PINEHURST COUNTRY CLUB NO. 3, PINEHURST, 1907 / PINEHURST COUNTRY CLUB NO. 4, PINEHURST, 1912 / PINEHURST COUNTRY CLUB NO. 5, PINEHURST,
OF SALISBURY, SALISBURY, 1927 / SEDGEFIELD COUNTRY CLUB, GREENSBORO, 1924 / SOUTHERN PINES COUNTRY CLUB, SOUTHERN PINES, 1923 / STRYKER GOLF CLU
1924 / *OHIO* / ACACIA COUNTRY CLUB, LYNDHURST, 1920 / ALADDIN COUNTRY CLUB, COLUMBUS, 1921 / ATHENS COUNTRY CLUB, ATHENS, 1921 / BROOKSIDE COUNTRY C
GOLF CLUB, DELAWARE, 1922 / ELKS COUNTRY CLUB OF COLUMBUS, COLUMBUS, 1921 / GRANVILLE GOLF CLUB, GRANVILLE, 1924 / HAMILTON ELKS COUNTRY CLUB, HAM
COUNTRY CLUB, LANCASTER, 1928 / MAKETEWAH COUNTRY CLUB, CINCINNATI, 1919 / MANAKIKI GOLF CLUB, WILLOUGHBY, 1928 / MIAMI SHORES GOLF CLUB, TROY, 19
1920 / PORTSMITH ELKS COUNTRY CLUB, MCDERMOTT, 1920 / SCIOTO COUNTRY CLUB, COLUMBUS, 1916 / SHAKER HEIGHTS COUNTRY CLUB, SHAKER HEIGHTS, 1913 /
GOLF COURSE, WORTHINGTON, 1922 / YOUNGSTOWN COUNTRY CLUB, YOUNGSTOWN, 1921 / ZANEVILLE COUNTRY CLUB, ZANEVILLE, 1932 / *PENNSYLVANIA* / ALLEGHENY
HILL FALLS, 1922 / CEDARBROOK COUNTRY CLUB, BLUE BELL, 1921 / EDGEWOOD COUNTRY CLUB, PITTSBURGH, 1921 / ELKVIEW GOLF CLUB, CARBONDALE, 1925 / GR
1923 / LEWISTOWN COUNTRY CLUB, LEWISTOWN, 1945 / LULU TEMPLE COUNTRY CLUB, NORTH HILLS, 1912 / OVERBROOK GOLF CLUB, PHILADELPHIA, 1922 / PHILADE
1945 / SILVERCREEK COUNTRY CLUB, HELLERTOWN, 1947 / ST. DAVIDS GOLF CLUB, WAYNE, 1927 / SUNNYBROOK COUNTRY CLUB, FLOURTOWN, 1921 / TORRESDALE F
COUNTRY CLUB OF YORK, YORK, 1927 / *RHODE ISLAND* / AGAWAM HUNT CLUB, RUMFORD, 1911 / METACOMET COUNTRY CLUB, EAST PROVIDENCE, 1921 / MISQ
WEST BARRINGTON, 1911 / SAKONNET GOLF CLUB, LITTLE COMPTON, 1921 / TRIGGS MEMORIAL GOLF CLUB, NORTH PROVIDENCE, 1930 / WANNAMOISETT COUNTRY CLU
1939 / FORT MILL GOLF CLUB, FORT MILL, 1947 / LANCASTER GOLF CLUB, LANCASTER, 1935 / *TENNESSEE* / BELLE MEADE COUNTRY CLUB, NASHVILLE, 1921 / BR
HILLS COUNTRY CLUB, KNOXVILLE, 1928 / MEMPHIS COUNTRY CLUB, MEMPHIS, 1910 / RICHLAND COUNTRY CLUB, NASHVILLE, 1920 / RIDGEFIELDS COUNTRY CLU
CLUB, HOUSTON, 1924 / SUNSET GROVE COUNTRY CLUB, ORANGE, 1923 / *VERMONT* / BURLINGTON COUNTRY CLUB, BURLINGTON, 1930 / WOODSTOCK COUNTRY CL
1912 / JEFFERSON-LAKESIDE COUNTRY CLUB, RICHMOND, 1921 / KINDERTON COUNTRY CLUB, CLARKSVILLE, 1947 / COUNTRY CLUB OF PETERSBURG, PETERSBUR
WESTWOOD GOLF CLUB, VIENNA, 1926 / WOODBURY FOREST GOLF CLUB, WOODBURY FOREST, 1910 / *WISCONSIN* / KENOSHA COUNTRY CLUB, KENOSHA, 1922 / OC
BANFF SPRINGS, 1912 / BRIGHTWOOD GOLF AND COUNTRY CLUB, DARTMOUTH, NOVA SCOTIA, 1934 / ESSEX GOLF AND COUNTRY CLUB, LASALLE, ONTARIO, 1929 /
919 / RIVERSIDE GOLF AND COUNTRY CLUB, NEW BRUNSWICK, 1937 / ROSEDALE GOLF CLUB, TORONTO, ONTARIO, 1919 / ROSELAND GOLF AND COUNTRY CLUB,